HARVARD STUDIES
IN INTERNATIONAL AFFAIRS
Number 43

THE DEPENDENCE DILEMMA:

Gasoline Consumption and America's Security

Edited by Daniel Yergin

Published by the
Center for International Affairs
Harvard University

THE DEPENDENCE DILEMMA:
Gasoline Consumption and America's Security

WITHDRAWN

CONTENTS

The Symposium on the Dependence Dilemma was held under the sponsorship of the International Energy Seminar at Harvard's Center for International Affairs. It took place at the Harvard Faculty Club on March 22, 1980. The Chairman was Daniel Yergin. Jacquie L. Kay was Coordinator.

ROBERT ALLEN, Lincoln, Mass.

ALVIN ALM, Fellow, Kennedy School of Government, Harvard University

MARTIN ANDERSEN, Transportation Systems Analyst, Transportation System Center, Department of Transportation, Cambridge, Mass.

JOHN ANDERSON, Senior Economic Analyst, Motor Vehicle Manufacturers, Washington, D.C.

GEORGE BABIKIAN, Senior Vice President, ARCO

STAN BENJAMIN, Energy Writer, Associated Press

DEBBIE BLEVIS, Federation of American Scientists, Washington, D.C.

JAMES BRUCE, Committee on Energy and Natural Resources, US Senate

CLARK BULLARD, Office of Technology Assessment, US Congress

JOHN R. BUNTING, Chairman Emeritus, First Pennsylvania Corporation

WILLIAM CHANDLER, Environmental Policy Institute, Washington, D.C.

JAMES CONSTANTINO, Director, Transportation System Center, Department of Transportation, Cambridge, Mass.

BEN COOPER, Committee on Energy and Natural Resources, US Senate

GARRY DeLOSS, Assistant Director, Conservation, Commonwealth of Massachusetts Energy Department, Boston, Mass.

NANCY DORFMAN, Research Associate, Center for Transportation Studies, Massachusetts Institute of Technology

S. R. DODSON, III, Coordinator of Strategic Planning, Exxon Chemical, Houston, Texas

LOUISE DUNLAP, Executive Vice-President, Environmental Policy Institute, Washington, D.C.

Professor JOHN KENNETH GALBRAITH, Harvard University

JONATHAN GIBSON, Sierra Club, Washington, D.C.

CHARLES GRAY, Chief, Emission Control Technology Division, Environmental Protection Agency, Ann Arbor, Michigan

WADE GREENE, New York, New York

Professor BRUCE HANNON, University of Illinois, Urbana, Ill.

ROBERTA HORNIG, Energy Writer, The Washington Star

DAVID HUNSBERGER, Management Consultant, Washington, D.C.

RICHARD JOHN, Director, Office of Energy and Environment, Transportation Systems Center, Department of Transportation, Cambridge, Mass.

CLIVE JONES, Energy Attaché, British Embassy, Washington, D.C.

JACQUIE KAY, Coordinator, Energy Symposium, Center for International Affairs, Harvard University

Professor HENRY W. KENDALL, Department of Physics, Massachusetts Institute of Technology

JONATHAN LASH, Natural Resources Development Council, Washington, D.C.

HENRY LEE, Executive Director, Energy and Environmental Policy Center, Kennedy School of Government, Harvard University

Professor CHARLES MAIER, Department of History, Duke University.

Professor TED MARMOR, School of Public Health, Yale University

JESSICA TUCHMAN MATHEWS, Editorial Page, The Washington Post

ALLAN McGOWAN, President, Scientists' Institute for Public Information, New York, New York

DAVID MELNIK, Energy Advisor, Province of Ontario, Canada

RICHARD MICHAELS, Director, Urban Systems Laboratory, University of Illinois, Chicago, Illinois

BRUCE MOHL, Boston Globe

Professor DENTON MORRISON, Department of Sociology, Michigan State University

MICHAEL MOSETTIG, Writer; Associate, The Columbia University School of Journalism

MITCHELL RESNICK, Business Week

ED ROBY, Energy Writer, United Press International

ROBERT ROSENBLATT, Energy Writer, Washington Bureau, Los Angeles Times

FRED SALVUCCI, Center for Transportation Studies, Massachusetts Institute of Technology

Professor THOMAS SCHELLING, Kennedy School of Government, Harvard University

WILLIAM SCHNEIDER, International Affairs Fellow, Council on Foreign Relations

DAVID SCHOOLER, Subcommittee on Energy and Power, Interstate and Foreign Commerce Committee, US House of Representatives

RUSSELL SCHWEICKART, Chairman, California Energy Commission, Sacramento, California

RICHARD SEXTRO, Lawrence-Berkeley Laboratory, University of California

RICHARD SHACKSON, Assistant Director for Transportation, Carnegie-Mellon Productivity Center

HERBERT SOSTEK, President, Gibbs Oil Company, Revere, Mass.

Professor ROBERT STOBAUGH, Harvard Business School

JAMES TANNER, Energy Writer, The Wall Street Journal

WILLIAM TAYLOR, Director, Office of Contingency Planning, Policy and Evaluation, Department of Energy, Washington, D.C.

DONALD TRILLING, Acting Director, Office of Inter-modal Transportation, Office of the Assistant Secretary, Policy and International Affairs, Department of Transportation, Washington, D.C.

MITCHELL TYSON, Office of Senator Paul Tsongas, US Senate

Professor FRANK VON HIPPEL, Center for Energy and Environmental Studies, Princeton University

H.L. WALTERS, Energy Planning Associate, Ford Motor Company

Professor ROBERT WILLIAMS, Center for Energy and Environmental Studies, Princeton University

Dr. DANIEL YERGIN, Center for International Affairs, Harvard University

Dr. DOROTHY ZINBERG, Center for Science and International Affairs, Harvard University

ACKNOWLEDGEMENTS

This Symposium was convened quickly, impelled by a strong sense of urgency brought about by the continuing pressures of the Second Oil Shock. Appreciation must be expressed, first, to those who wrote papers, gave presentations, and attended — all on short notice.

I want to thank Professor Samuel Huntington, Director of the Center for International Affairs, for his encouragement of the undertaking. I also want to thank Professor Joseph Nye for his advice and support. Dr. Grant Hammond, Executive Officer of the Center, devoted a great deal of effort to making the Symposium a success.

It was Mr. Robert Allen whose fundamental concern, dedication, and commitment made the Symposium possible. Mr. Wade Greene, sharing in the sense of urgency, also played a key role in shaping the Symposium. I am deeply grateful to both of them.

Special appreciation must be expressed to Dr. Jacquie Kay. Her formidable organizational abilities — combined with her enthusiasm and persuasiveness — were essential to the successful outcome of the Symposium. It was a pleasure to work with her.

Chris McKay, Ann Stibal, and Leslie Sterling provided important assistance.

Peter Jacobsohn, The Editor of the Center's publications, again proved what a scrutinizing and discriminating editor he is, and his care helped shape this book. Finally, Jane Shorall, a skilled and talented editor, coordinated and organized this publication—a demanding task carried out with verve. I thank them both.

Daniel Yergin
Cambridge, Mass.
June 1980

PART I

_____ OVERVIEW

by Daniel Yergin

The United States finds itself increasingly challenged in the
world today. Its foreign policy is constrained, its influence and
security position eroding, its economy vulnerable, its alliance
relations under pressure. Among the most important reasons —
perhaps even the most important — is the over-dependence on
insecure imported oil. The reverberations of this over-
dependence are directly felt in American foreign policy and
throughout the economic and political system. Thus, there is a
fundamental relation between America's problems in the world,
and how 140 million vehicles are used on the nation's roads and
highways.

For a quarter century, motoring in America was a dream. The
real price of gasoline went down; new highways were spun out
of the highway trust fund; and the suburban living pattern
provided an incentive for — and depended upon — the automobile. So, when buying a new car, the American motorist could
well afford to content himself with considering options and
performance and design. One thing the motorist obviously did
not need to worry about was gasoline, for gasoline was cheap,
and easily available.

Times have changed. In the 1970s, motorists ran into gas lines,
shortages, and erratic price movements. Gasoline was no longer
cheap, nor could one assume that it was easily available.

There are good reasons to think that the problems gasoline
shortages created during the 1970s were but previews of the
coming attractions of the 1980s — not in every year, but at
various times, depending on the condition of the world oil
market and political developments in oil-producing regions.
The constraints on oil, which many Americans experienced as
gas lines, are likely to become more pronounced in this decade.
And in the 1980s, those constraints may give rise to sharp security crises as well as to deteriorating economic conditions.

Through most of the 1970s, the American political process
refused to acknowledge the connection between US domestic
energy policies, on the one hand, and world politics and the
international position of the United States, on the other. Yet the
connection is intimate, and is tied up with threats to America's

over-all well-being. America's domestic energy situation — and the extent of US dependence on imports — could be just as important, if not more important, in shaping the future political configurations in the Persian Gulf — and our future welfare — than direct security policies. For American oil consumption has a profound influence on the world. The United States is, in effect, the Saudi Arabia of consumption. It uses almost a third of all the oil consumed in the world every day. US imports were 3.4 million barrels a day in 1970; they have risen to 8-8.5 mb/d, and today the United States has become the largest importer of oil in the world, the largest buyer of OPEC petroleum. Almost half of American oil today is imported, compared to a quarter in 1970.

Within that context, American gasoline consumption — more than a third of America's over-all oil consumption — has particular importance. The US runs on gasoline; liquid fuels are the hub of the complex of issues known as the energy problem; yet transportation is also the consumption area where it is most difficult to substitute non-oil fuels. At the same time, US gasoline consumption is a profoundly important part of the world oil market. One of every nine barrels of oil used in the world every day is burned as gasoline on American highways. US gasoline consumption alone is larger than any other country's entire oil consumption. This is not a moral judgement. It is simply a statement of fact — and of scale. Yet there may well be much greater flexibility in how we use gasoline in America than is generally believed.

A reduction in US gasoline consumption offers a number of important benefits. First, it would reduce the number of dollars flowing out of the United States under the current OPEC pricing system. Second, it would change the balance in the world oil market, help to cap prices, and be a major step toward bringing inflation under control. Third, it would reduce the pressure on certain key producers. Fourth, it would increase our margin of safety when the next "accident" interrupts part of the flow of oil. Fifth, it would provide more flexibility for US foreign policy, both in "normal" times and in a crisis. Sixth, it would much increase American credibility in dealing with its allies. The significance of that last problem has been made clear in the stresses in Western relations produced by the Iranian hostage crisis. The US has asked other countries to join in sanctions against Iran. These countries have, in turn, inquired how the United States might make up for the oil they import from Iran that would be jeopardized. The obvious answer is by reducing our demand, thereby freeing oil for the world market. That would have required certain demand restraint policies in the United States. The requisite steps, at least in the first six months of the Embassy seizure, were not carried out.

The reasons do not end there. In what is likely to be the gloomy context of an even more unstable and unpredictable world oil supply system, a reshaping of US gasoline consumption could do a great deal to reduce or prevent painful conflict and crises.

What would be a reasonable target for reducing demand? A working assumption might be a reduction in gasoline demand on the order of 1.5 to 2 million barrels a day—amounting to a reduction of 20 to 25 percent in gasoline use. In other sectors of the economy, this has been the range of energy savings achieved with relatively minor efforts and relatively small penalties. No one can say with any confidence how easy or how difficult reaching this target would prove to be. However, the experience of the last six years indicates that setting significant targets is a constructive practice. Achieving this goal would have the same effect as adding, at current export levels, a new Kuwait—or a new Iran—to the world oil market.

The fact that we have moved into a protracted energy emergency since January 1979 certainly strengthens the case for the 1.5 to 2 million barrel a day target. Our over-dependence on oil creates a new situation in American history, and translates into extreme vulnerability, whether measured in economic or political terms, or in terms of military security. The economic dangers have been dramatized by recent events. The weekly bill for US oil imports rose from $800 million a week at the end of 1978 to $1.8 billion by March 1980, creating a hurricane force behind inflation and imposing a grave penalty on economic activity. The Iranian hostage crisis shows how hamstrung American foreign policy and American influence in the world have become with the transfer of so much political power into the hands of oil producers. It is deeply troubling—to our allies as well—to see the United States so immobilized and isolated. Our foreign policy has become hostage, not only to various producers' rational foreign policy goals, but also to the whims, ambitions, and paranoid fantasies of other groups. Such is the consequence of our over-dependence in the context of the current oil market.

A substantial reduction in US oil imports would have a liberating and invigorating effect for America's overall international position. The security threat is manifold: interruption of supplies, sudden regime shifts, the rise of "hostile oil" (petroleum produced by countries antagonistic to the West), Soviet

adventurism, and collisions over oil and oil-related issues with
our most important allies. Here, too, we are much more secure if
we reduce our dependence on foreign oil and thus the pressure
on the world market. This would not, of course, make these
problems disappear. But we would have a much better chance of
dealing with them, of mitigating and even avoiding some difficulties by, for instance, reducing the pressure on those oil-
producing states whose interests are closest to our own. We
would increase our credibility and our flexibility for what will
be the inevitable oil crises of the 1980s. In sum, America's
over-dependence on imported oil has been one of the main
factors in shaping an international oil market that is highly
detrimental to US interests, thus sharply accentuating US security problems. This over-dependence puts the United States into
a position where it could be drawn into the vortex of a crisis with
little choice or little maneuverability. Hence the dependence
dilemma.

Few people would argue against the desirability of reducing
US gasoline consumption from its current level of seven million
barrels a day to 5 or 5.5 mb/d, yet there is substantial disagreement as to how to achieve it. Part of that disagreement arises
from the considerable confusion and uncertainty concerning
the various options. In an effort to deal with this quandary and
to contribute to the process of understanding and decision, the
International Energy Seminar at Harvard's Center for International Affairs convened its symposium on the Dependence Dilemma. At first glance, this might seem an unusual subject for a
seminar and a Center dealing with international affairs. But two
of the consistent themes of the seminar over the last several
years have been the importance of demand management and the
inseparability of domestic US energy policy and international
issues. The events of the Second Oil Shock following the revolution in Iran—including the doubling of the price of oil to levels
not expected until the year 2000—have dramatized those two
themes. The likelihood of supply interruptions and new constraints on world oil provided a strong sense of urgency—made
even stronger by the fear that a failure to think through the
gasoline issue now could prove very costly to the nation in the
near future.

What follows is an edited transcript of the Symposium, plus
papers and comments written for the conference. In sum they
provide rich insights into the potential—and the difficulties—
inherent in the various alternatives.

The conference was not meant to arrive at any specific recommendations and conclusions. But, at least to this participant, certain themes emerged as paramount.

1. The outlook for oil supplies in the 1980s is likely to worsen.

Despite efficiency gains in transportation and other sectors, US oil imports are likely to increase in the 1980s. It is generally assumed that, even with the stimulation of decontrol, domestic US oil production is likely to fall during the decade by three to four million barrels a day. One forecast presented at the conference suggested that, without further efforts to stimulate conservation, US oil imports could rise from 8-8.5 million barrels a day to 10 mb/d by 1985. Synthetic fuels are unlikely to have any noticeable impact until the middle 1990s at the earliest. On top of this, oil producers are likely to restrict production in order to keep prices moving up. A number of oil producers are vulnerable to internal upheavals that could interrupt production; and a Soviet quest for influence over the Persian Gulf now seems increasingly pronounced. Thus, there is a compelling need for a more accelerated effort to reduce petroleum consumption in the United States.

Virtually all American gasoline is produced in American refineries. Would a reduction in demand of 1.5 to 2 mb/d create inordinate problems for the American refining industry? On the contrary, a number of speakers pointed out, it would make refining life easier. Refineries have to work quite hard to take a barrel that comes in containing 20 percent gasoline and work it into a product slate that is 50 percent gasoline. As heavier crudes become relatively more important, the industry is faced with the need to make very large capital investments. If demand for gasoline were reduced, they would not have to undertake this heavy investment program.

2. Higher post-1985 automobile efficiency standards are probably necessary to ensure the nation's mobility.

Without the current standards, Detroit might well have been less prepared for the sudden surge in 1979 of demand for more fuel efficient vehicles. Standards provide the industry with some security in the face of potentially volatile consumer demand, yet also allow the industry a good deal of flexibility. Many participants thought that post-1985 standards—up to 40 miles per gallon—were necessary to help maintain a viable American auto industry. At the same time, it was recognized that the real barrier for Detroit is the enormous amount of capital required to meet those standards—increasingly difficult to assemble as foreign auto makers take a larger share of the domestic market. The marshalling of those resources is not only a challenge for the American auto industry, but also for American society. One participant suggested, as a rough guide, that a capital investment to save an additional two to three million barrels a day by 1995 might be about the same as the capital investment required to produce two to three million barrels a day in a synthetic fuels program. In his paper, Frank von Hippel pointed to two important considerations. First, there is a significant shortfall between EPA test performances and actual highway driving. Second, even though gasoline prices go up, the increasing fuel efficiency of cars means that motorists will not see a sharp rise in cents per mile. The post-1985 standards will not be made redundant by rising gas prices, but rather standards and gasoline prices (including tax) will reinforce energy efficiency.

3. The United States is woefully unprepared for a supply interruption.

One may not be able to predict the causes now, but one or more significant supply interruptions in the next few years are highly probable. The United States, despite two oil shocks, is not ready. The strategic petroleum reserve, far from having the equivalent of 180 days of imports called for under America's International Energy Agency agreements, has the equivalent of only 11 days of imports, and it is not expected to have any additional fill until 1981. High interest rates will cause companies to run down their current high level of private stocks, which are an important buffer. The stand-by emergency rationing plan could probably not be applied in an emergency in an effective and timely manner.

In his paper, Alvin Alm proposed what could be a much more effective emergency plan. In a supply interruption, prices would be allowed to rise right away. Ninety percent of the rise above a base price would be captured in a windfall tax and rebated. Such a plan would involve far less bureaucracy than a rationing plan.

4. The distinction between emergency responses and preventive steps is difficult to make.

The United States might be forced to seek to curtail consumption in a supply interruption. It also has a compelling interest in reducing demand to help keep the price of oil from rising as well as to help shape a market in which an upheaval is likely to have significant effects. Moreover, the options are just about the same. Van pooling is a way to reduce gasoline consumption under any circumstances. Fred Salvucci stressed a very important point: these alternatives take time to start up; therefore, you want them in place before a crisis. In other words, what is useful in an emergency is what is also useful as a conserving tool.

Some argue that the United States should not try to reduce demand—except in an emergency—so that there is "fat to cut out of the system." This is clearly a highly flawed argument. It ignores both the effect of US consumption on the world market, and the cost to the nation of high level imports which drive up prices, and also distort the demand and supply situation. Moreover, by this logic, the United States should seek to increase its consumption by three million barrels a day so that it would have more fat to cut out during the next emergency!

5. Rationing could be much more difficult to implement than is widely thought.

A close look at rationing leads to increasing wariness. There is a tendency to think that its practicality and ease were demonstrated in World War II, and that it is inherently equitable. Both propositions are questionable. As Professor Galbraith and Michael Mosettig suggest, the circumstances of World War II rationing were much different from today—a much smaller auto population, major mass transit alternatives, and a high degree of national solidarity (only six critical articles in the major magazines during the entire war!). Rationing appears equitable until one gets into the question of how exceptions will be granted, and the complicated procedures that will ensue—in effect, draft boards for the entire driving population. Meanwhile, what is equitable to a driver in New Jersey is quite different from what is equitable to a driver in Wyoming.

The potential administrative nightmare is suggested in both William Chandler's and Alvin Alm's papers. If ration coupons are distributed on the basis of car registration, then questions arise both about junkers and the delays in getting registrations on the rolls. If rationing is done on the basis of license holders, one might expect an additional 30 million people to register for licenses. A substantial number of people might not receive their entitlement vouchers in the mail. Gas lines could be replaced by coupon lines, as people queue up to exchange their entitlement vouchers for coupons. The current rationing proposals involve a white market—that is, people will be able to buy and sell coupons. In effect, a second currency will be created—one in which there will be at least as many physical notes in circulation as the first—potentially a considerable headache.

In this regard, Thomas Schelling's very thoughtful and incisive analysis of the equity questions leads to the conclusion that things may not be quite what they seem—or rather, that things that seem quite different are not so different. To compare a rationing/white market scheme with a gas tax/rebate scheme would appear to involve a comparison between apples and oranges. In fact, underneath somewhat different skins, they may all be apples.

As Schelling points out, the price of gasoline may be $1.50, and the market value of the coupons 50 cents. So when the motorist pulls up to buy, say, one gallon, he is paying $1.50 for each gallon and handing over a coupon provided by the government, which has a market value of 50 cents. He is actually, therefore, paying $2.00 a gallon, but the last 50 cents is given to him by the government. This is not much different from a tax with a rebate where the pump price is $2.00—$1.50 plus 50 cents tax—and the government sends the motorist not a coupon worth 50 cents, but a 50 cent piece as a rebate. And, in this way, we can stick with one currency, rather than create a second.

The question, of course, is consistently and fairly asked—"What about lower income groups, the poor?" This issue should not be brushed aside with simple reference to the virtues of prices as regulators of demand, as some attempt to do. A number of participants addressed this question directly. There is little doubt that oil price controls have favored the well-off; lower income groups have proportionately fewer cars and drive less. Schelling made the strong point that it does not make a great deal of sense to design an energy policy primarily to meet the needs of a small minority. Much better to frame an energy policy that serves national goals, and to design specific programs to relieve the problems of lower income groups. Rebate proposals, for instance, could be quite progressive, favoring those on lower incomes. A broader point should be made as well: lower income groups in the United States have been hurt much more by $30 a barrel oil and its consequences—inflation and recession—than they would have been by the changes in price in the years 1974-78 that might have prevented US gasoline demand from surging 10 percent ahead at exactly the time the Shah fell and the Second Oil Shock began.

6. A gas tax might protect the interest of the motorist in maintaining mobility more effectively than rationing.

In other countries, a gasoline tax is accepted as a normal mode of taxation, as these figures indicate:

Tax on Regular Gasoline
Early 1980
(US dollars/US gallon)

US	0.14
France	1.62
Italy	1.83
West Germany	1.14

In the United States, the political process has gone to great lengths and contortions to avoid considering a gas tax, even though the federal highway tax has since 1969 been eroded 60 percent by inflation. But such a tax may be an efficient way to reshape demand in a highly flexible way, depending on how it is structured. Robert Williams, in his paper, proposed a $2 a gallon tax, with the proceeds to be rebated in a progressive fashion. Others argued for a tax shift. Gasoline has increased in relative scarcity value. Tax it, but reduce the tax in other areas, such as Social Security or income tax. There is not sufficient data to predict by how much demand will be reduced under these circumstances. However, it has been suggested that, if a tax were presented as a *conservation* device, and thus the "signal" were reinforced, the tax need. not be at a penalty level to have a substantial constructive effect on demand. Indeed, a basic choice can be discerned. If demand in the United States goes unchecked, circumstances are created in which OPEC can sharply increase what amounts to its tax on the American consumer—a tax that is *not* rebated. Or the United States can tax itself, keep the money in the United States, and rebate it to consumers. The most desirable circumstances—to go "tax free"—is no longer possible in the current configuration of the world oil market.

7. There might be much greater flexibility in how people use their cars than the conventional wisdom would tell us.

The customary notion has it that the only way conservation can come is through improved miles per gallon. But current research strongly suggests that there are other promising ways. Richard Michaels points out that such methods as trip planning and better selection of daily routes could, at least on the basis of preliminary research, bring savings in the range of 15 to 30 percent. Similarly, Fred Salvucci, drawing on the research at MIT's Transportation Center, points to savings in that range resulting from better maintenance and correct tire pressure and ridesharing. In particular, car-pooling and, even more so, van-pooling based on the workplace could deliver a great deal of conservation. Indeed, employers may become more involved in getting their employees to work—a fringe benefit like meals in the cafeteria. There are conservation measures that may be used to reshape demand to help head off an emergency—or to help us get through an emergency.

8. Polls indicate that public opinion is shifting toward much stronger support for conservation—but. . .

No one, least of all an elected official, should fail to note that a gas tax would be less than universally popular, at least initially. There is a gap between public perceptions and careful analysis of what may be required to assure the American people their mobility in the 1980s. In his paper, William Schneider points out that the public favors rationing not because it likes rationing, but because it perceives rationing as preferable to gas lines. He suggests that the public might have to experience rationing to decide that it prefers a gas tax. Of course, public cynicism and skepticism also come into play—beginning with the doubts about the energy problem. Moreover, the public could suspect that a gas tax would be enacted—and then the rebate or tax shift conveniently forgotten. Therefore, the rebate or tax shift might need to be enacted first. Ted Marmor points out a basic distinction: the real implementation problem for a gasoline tax is getting it enacted. For rationing, it is not the enacting, but rather actually doing the rationing.

Fairness is a basic question. People want a system that is fair. Unfortunately, fairness can be in the eye of the beholder. Moreover, the appearance of fairness may prove quite different from the reality. In an effort to reconcile different interests, and to guarantee a basic allotment, John Kenneth Galbraith proposed that everyone receive a basic allotment of gasoline stamps, ensuring everyone at least a base, and the rest to be bought at a high price. This would be a kind of insurance, and could respond to people's fear of "being had."

Many contradictory pressures will shape what the United States does—or does not do—about gasoline consumption and oil imports. It is such pressures that help create the dependence dilemma. In such circumstances, the most practical way to proceed might be something like this: The current US tax level (without the new import fee) is about less than ten percent sixth of the average gasoline tax of France, Germany, and Italy. As already noted, given inflation, that level is actually lower in real terms than when it was first enacted in 1955. An additional tax of 30 to 50 cents could be added—bringing the level to one-third to one-half the average level of those three Western European countries. It would clearly be stressed that this is a conservation tax. It might be specifically dedicated to four vital needs: to provide incentives to the American people for conservation investments; to help the auto industry meet the awesome capital requirements imposed by the rapid adaptation to oil constraints; to finance tax rebates and tax shifts; to help vitalize mass transit and other alternatives to the single-passenger trip (e.g., credits to businesses that provide van-pooling). This tax might be increased in real terms by increments of 10 to 15 cents a gallon a year over the next five years—giving a very clear and timely signal.

Beyond that, we should not be dependent *only* on a standby rationing plan. There should also be a standby emergency tax plan, perhaps in the form outlined in the Alm paper.

What emerges is that there is no perfect option. We are a society that depends on a high degree of mobility. Our over-dependence on an international energy system that is crisis-prone and accident-prone could create a crisis of mobility in this country in the 1980s. Our over-dependence itself is a profound pressure on that system and, indeed, constitutes a threat to American security. Despite six and a half years and two oil shocks, we have hardly begun to take those steps that are so manifestly in our own interest, and indeed required in the name of elemental self-preservation.

Table I

Oil—1979

(million barrels per day)

	Total Consumption	Net Imports
United States	18.8	7.8
Japan	5.1	5.6
France	2.1	2.4
United Kingdom	1.7	.4
West Germany	2.7	2.8

Source: *International Energy Statistical Review,*
    Energy Information Administration

Table II

Gasoline Consumption 1978

	mb/d	barrels gasoline/ per capita
United States	7.5	12.3
Western Europe	2.4	—
France	.4	2.8
West Germany	.5	3.2
United Kingdom	.4	2.6
Japan	.6	1.8

Derived from: Department of Energy, *International Petroleum Annual 1978*

Table III

U.S. Motor Gasoline Supplied and Production

(millions of barrels per day)

	1978			1979			1980		
	Total Motor Gasoline Supplied	Unleaded Gasoline Supplied	Production	Total Motor Gasoline Supplied	Unleaded Gasoline Supplied	Production	Total Motor Gasoline Supplied	Unleaded Gasoline Supplied	Production
Jan	6.7	2.1	6.9	6.9	2.6	7.3	7.0	2.9	6.3
Feb	6.9	2.2	6.6	7.3	2.7	6.9	6.6	3.0	6.9
Mar	7.3	2.4	6.8	7.2	2.7	6.7			
Apr	7.2	2.4	6.7	7.1	2.8	6.8			
May	7.7	2.3	7.1	7.2	2.8	6.8			
Jun	7.9	2.7	7.2	7.2	2.8	7.0			
Jul	7.6	2.6	7.3	6.9	2.8	7.0			
Aug	7.9	2.8	7.5	7.3	3.0	6.9			
Sep	7.4	2.6	7.4	6.8	2.8	6.6			
Oct	7.5	2.6	7.2	7.0	2.8	6.5			
Nov	7.5	2.7	7.6	6.8	2.9	6.7			
Dec	7.5	2.8	7.8	6.7	2.9	7.0			

Source: Energy Information Administration,
Weekly Petroleum Status Report

Table IV

Distribution of US Gasoline
Consumption—1977

	Percent
Autos	72.6
Motorcycles	0.4
Buses	0.4
Single Unit Trucks	23.8
General Aviation	0.4
Water Transport	0.7
Other	1.7
	100

Source: *Transportation Energy
Conservation Data Book,*
Third Edition, 2-15

Table V

Principal Means of
Transportation to Work
in the US, 1976
(percent)

	Total	In Central Cities
Total Car	88.9	79.6
(Drives self)	(72.9)	(66.9)
(Car pools)	(16.0)	(12.7)
Mass Transportation	5.6	13.4
Bicycle or Motorcycle	0.8	1.0
Taxicab	0.2	0.4
Walks only	4.0	5.1
Other Means	0.6	0.6

Source: *Transportation Energy Conservation Data Book,*
        Third Edition, 1-118

PART II

The Symposium began with an overview of the issues. "The number one problem facing the country is the energy problem, and the number one part of that is gasoline consumption," said Robert Stobaugh of the Harvard Business School. "American gasoline consumption accounts for about one out of every nine barrels of oil produced in the entire world. It is larger in volume than any other country's entire oil consumption.

"Three myths are now beginning to circulate. One is that we have already done a great job of conserving and, therefore don't have to worry about any more conservation. That myth applies especially to gasoline. We hear figures that demand near the end of last year and early part of this year was down about 10 percent from year earlier periods. That is said to be proof that the price mechanism is working. Indeed, I have even seen elasticity estimates — estimates of the public's responsiveness to changes in price — showing how well it's working.

"I would say that that conclusion is really quite premature for several reasons. In the early part of 1979, gasoline demand was running very, very high, an all-time record for that particular time of the year. So we have a bench mark that's higher than normal. We also have a number of things occurring simultaneously. So we cannot really tell how much of that is due to other factors and how much of the consumption drop-off is due to price. For one thing, there are mandatory mileage regulations on automobiles, which means the fleet average is beginning to get more efficient. Secondly, there is a residual thought in people's minds that maybe they should not use so much gasoline because of a fear of shortage, especially as they remember the gasoline lines from last spring. I would guess the more time people have between them and last summer, the less that memory will impact on their gasoline usage. Thirdly, in some parts of the country, Florida especially, they are beginning to have gasoline shortages right now so that people are afraid to take a long trip because they are afraid they cannot get gasoline.

"So for these reasons, I think it's much too early to start drawing firm conclusions about price elasticities for gasoline. After we have gone in and out of the recession — then we can begin to get some kind of a measure as to how important this price effect has been.

"The second myth is that of an oil glut. Now that we are getting into a recession here — and perhaps a little later in Europe and Japan — and now that we have relatively calm conditions in the international oil market, it's inevitable that the spot price of crude oil will begin to come down. And of course, it has been quite volatile in the past, both on the up and the down side. I would say, do not be misled by talk of an oil glut. Drops in the spot prices of oil will be part of a lull that is likely to occur between now and the time we begin to pull out of a recession.

"The third myth that I have been hearing lately is 'Let's not conserve now, so when we do get into problems several years from now, there will be more fat to cut out of the system.' If we believe that kind of logic, we should go back and replay the first quarter of 1979. I would say that if we had actually reduced the fat between 1973 and 1979 and if US gasoline consumption had been substantially lower and oil imports substantially lower, then we would not have had the run-up in world oil prices that we saw during 1979. We would have substantially lower oil prices on the world market than we have now — as well as substantially better economic conditions in the United States.

"One of the lessons of 1979 is that, during a relatively tight market, a very small shortage can cause very chaotic conditions in supply and on the price front. I would not like to go into the next accident we might have with a tight market, operating on the theory that we can always cut out a couple of million barrels a day if we have to."

Mr. Stobaugh went on to point out the two important issues regarding the oil problem. "One is the fear of a sudden cutoff and, therefore, the need to develop emergency plans that can be implemented fairly quickly. That is essential. If you go back and review the history of world oil prices over the last 30 years, you find that generally the upward price movements have been a result of accidents and unforeseen events that have happened in one form or another that have impacted on the world oil supply and on oil prices. Nobody can predict when we are going to have another one of these unforeseen events. It's anybody's guess about where and when it might occur.

"Another reason why emergency plans are important is because we have not been moving ahead very quickly with putting oil into the strategic reserve. Compounding the inventory problem are the high interest rates. A number of oil companies are deliberately running down their oil inventories because of the tremendous cost of working capital. You start paying 18 or 19 or 20 percent to carry your oil inventories, and you find that you can work with fewer days of inventories than you ordinarily might do. Unless there is a substantial drop in interest rates, we are likely to see a run-down in inventories held by oil companies during this coming year. That, coming together with the fact that we do not have that much oil in strategic reserve, means that emergency plans are even more important.

"The other issue is that of lowering normal usage. We not only have the impact that that might make on a long-run tightness and price in the world oil market, but also that it would free up the market some so that we could begin to put oil into the strategic reserve. Of course, the outflow of funds from the US compounds the economic growth issues and the higher oil prices compound the inflation issues.

"We do have econometric models that say, here is how much of inflation is due to energy prices. These models are not very good because they do not make sufficient allowance for the indirect effects of the demand for higher wages brought about because people see that they are paying more for gasoline and heating oil. So we have energy impacting on inflation.

"Finally, there is the national security issue. Oil is at the center of that. I don't think anybody foresees that we are going to have more stability in the Middle East in the future than we have had in the past. If you relive the history of the Middle East, you see how frequently there have been upsets. Moreover, since the end of 1979 we have had the problem of the Soviets getting much more aggressive in the Middle East, in particular by their move into Afghanistan. Related to that question is how important and how necessary will imported oil be to the Soviets and their allies during the mid-1980s.

"Gasoline is especially important to this whole question of oil imports and national security because many people think gasoline can be reduced more than some of the other oil products with less effect on GNP. In other words, some people think that you can more easily reduce gasoline consumption a million and a half to two million barrels a day than you could other oil consumption — and with less impact on economic conditions and economic growth.

"The other thing related to the national security issues is the great political importance that gasoline demand in the United States has in our dealing with allies. Almost every time I talk with a European, one of the first things they focus on is what they see as an enormous hemorrhage in the world oil system that has been taking place on the American highway through our gasoline consumption."

"We don't see that there is an absolute shortage of energy

coming down the pike," said Samuel Dodson of Exxon. "We think we're moving toward a period where it will be harder and more costly to get this energy into usable form. But we don't see an absolute shortage. Liquids are the critical factor in this transition period.

"That, however, does lead us to somewhat of an anomaly in focusing on motor gasoline. While most people in this room perceive motor gasoline as a luxury good, one in which changes can be made relatively easily and at low cost, the transportation sector is the area in which there are the most difficulties in substituting other types of fuel. A lot of the evidence indicates that it's much cheaper and much easier to find substitutes for other parts of the barrel than for motor gasoline. The options for people who burn heavy fuel oil, who burn home heating oil, are greater than the options for people who are using gasoline. It boils down to the fact that in the case of gasoline and diesel fuel today the only real options are on the conservation side. There are no other fuels that are readily available to substitute here.

"Our forecast shows a significant drop in gasoline demand in the US over the next 20 years. We are forecasting a drop from about seven and a half million barrels a day of motor gasoline demand in 1978 to about four and a half million barrels a day in the year 2000. This is a fairly significant drop, larger than what most people are forecasting.

"There are a number of ways of getting from A to B and obviously one of the things we want to talk about today is how we get there, whether we do it through the price mechanism or through a regulatory mechanism.

"In looking at how we get there, I would close with three thoughts. One is we ought to make sure that we look at the cost to the economy of getting there. The second is we ought to make sure that we are not buying conservation that costs us more than the alternate fuel that can be produced domestically.

"Finally, one of the critical issues today is how fast we make this transition. Do we want to try to do it today? Is that a more costly way or is it a cheaper way than to try to do it over a 20-year period?

"The way that we happen to have gotten to our four and a half million barrels a day is an assumption that people continue to drive more and more. Today the average licensed driver drives about 7700 miles a year. Our forecast assumes he is going to drive about 10,000 miles a year in the year 2000. That's about a one-third increase. We are assuming he's going to drive a car that has a fleet average in 2000 of about 33 or 34 miles per gallon and a new car average of about 37 miles per gallon. We are assuming that about 5 percent of new cars will be electric cars in the year 2000, although that may be a very pessimistic assumption.

"In essence we have opted for an assumption that says that the long-range trend of people driving more and more is going to continue.

"That's not necessarily the only way for this to happen. It can easily happen that people drive the same or less or opt for bigger cars or other things like that. But our forecast is premised upon increasing saturation of the population of licensed drivers, an increase from today's rate in the amount of miles he drives, and a continuing mix or shift toward higher mileage cars."

"Your forecast is also based on tremendous substitution of diesel oil for gasoline," Mr. Stobaugh noted, "so that your over-all estimate of transportation consumption goes up in the year 2000. If you look only at gasoline, you're getting only a partial picture."

"We are forecasting a decline in total motor fuel demands," replied Dodson. "But nothing like from 7 down to 4.5, that is true."

George Babikian, senior vice-president of marketing for ARCO, noted that his firm had just completed forecasts to the year 2000. "It highlights the problem we face in 1985 in this country, not the problem we face in 1980 or 1990 or the year 2000," he said.

"If we remain with President Carter's import limit of 8.2 million barrels a day net, we are going to have a shortfall of something like two million barrels a day in this country by the year 1986. We either are going to have to import two million barrels a day more than that limit or we are going to have to do without. Now, in Exxon's study, the assumption is made that this country will import whatever crude it needs to satisfy our energy needs. I hope we don't do that. I'm not making that comment from a strategic point of view, although I think that's a very valid reason why we shouldn't gear imports to our needs. Certainly the strategic aspects can't be discounted. I'm making that comment from a purely economic point of view. Importing 10 million barrels a day of foreign oil would put very onerous economic burdens on the country. I'm not even sure we could afford it. Our import bill this year is going to be somewhere between 90 to 95 billion dollars, depending on which number you want to believe. The latest forecast for our balance of pay-ments deficit is going to be something like $15 billion if these projections are correct. And if you add another two million barrels on that some time in the next five years, the impact is going to be far more than just the effect of that two million barrels. If the oil exporting countries realize that we are that much more dependent on their product, I think their price is going to be raised differentially.

"From an economic point of view we have got to keep our imports at no more than this 8.2 million level, perhaps even less. I think it can be done without a great deal of sacrifice on the part of the people in this country. Conservation is really the main ingredient in the formula to cut our demand down for this imported oil during this short period of time.

"Maybe we will be lucky and find oil in some field that will allow us to bring that oil to market quickly. But I doubt it. The reason we are going to be more dependent on foreign oil than we originally thought is not because of demand, for demand isn't going up that much between now and 1986; rather, it is because domestic production will be going down precipitously.

"Earlier estimates made about our capabilities of producing domestic crudes, have to be, at least at this point, regarded as exaggerated. I hope I'm wrong, but I don't think so. It is the prediction our people are making."

There was a disagreement among the Symposium's participants, however, as to whether the effects of higher mileage cars will be as great as some forecasts showed. "In fact, the fuel economy of new cars has been improving," said Frank von Hippel of Princeton, "but not as much as Congress wanted, and not as much as it appears that events require. One of the problems has been the yardstick by which buyers chose to measure fuel economy. The EPA yardstick was the only yardstick we had. For the more fuel-efficient cars, which are being mandated for 1985, the yardstick turns out to have been shrinking. The cars which measure 27½ mpg in the EPA test, on average get only 20 miles a gallon on the road or even less. So the improvement isn't enough."

Other forecasts suggest higher levels of imports despite greater fuel efficiency. While reduction in gasoline demand might have only a limited or even no impact on economic growth, some have argued that that kind of reduction would have such significant negative impact on the refining industry as to create serious obstacles. This proposition was, however, rejected. "I don't really think there will be any serious dislocation as a result of significant conservation in gasoline use," said Babikian. "Units that today produce gasoline wouldn't be run or would be switched to distillate production. Also the industry will back out crude, imported crude, and make the investment in cokers and other cracking units to upgrade the bottom of the barrel. Backing out crude will have a mitigating effect on surplus inventories and upgrading residual petroleum will have a beneficial energy effect.

"Refineries swing from maximum gasoline production to maximum distillate production depending on the time of year. There is a capability of anywhere from 5 to 10 percent switch depending on the refinery. The first thing that would happen with a 5 to 10 percent reduction in gasoline demand would be a switch to maximizing distillate. Our projections for the 1980s indicate distillate volumes are going to grow fairly significantly — about 35 percent, so we will need the distillate. By putting in more cokers, we can satisfy this additional distillate demand by cracking residual fuel and thus back out crude — imported crude. Residual fuel will be in ample supply and by "cracking" resid, 75 percent of it can be converted to distillate or gasoline. Today resid is used basically as boiler fuel or asphalt. It will be more valuable as distillate."

"A good way to conceptualize what goes on in the refinery," said Mr. Stobaugh, "is that crude oil comes in with a natural stream in it containing 20 percent gasoline on the average. Now, in the United States, that crude is worked on until you get up to 50 percent gasoline on the average. So if you wanted to cut it down to 40 or 30, you might idle some units or operate them differently, but it would not cause you fundamental problems. If you want to go down to 15 percent or 10 percent, then you'd have problems. But we don't see anything like going that low in sight."

"Would it really back out any imported oil or simply show up as some other product?" asked Stan Benjamin of the Associated Press."

"Our best chance of backing out imported oil is to have a reduction in gasoline demand," said Babikian.

WILL WE HAVE AUTO FUEL EFFICIENCY STANDARDS AFTER 1985?

We are now more than halfway along the efficiency track decreed by Congress in 1975. By 1985, the fleet average is supposed to have doubled to 27.5 miles per gallon. But what about after 1985? The question of post-1985 auto standards is already moving to the fore as a subject of major debate. The issue arises at a time when the American automobile industry is under heavy pressure from foreign — principally Japanese — competition.

Some argue that additional standards would make any further financial measures, such as a tax, irrelevant. Others take the opposite position — that price levels likely to prevail then would make additional standards unnecessary. The subject provoked considerable discussion at the Symposium. Generally, there was a tendency to accept the need for stronger post-1985 standards. Frank von Hippel argued that standards need to be pushed to the 40 to 50 mpg level by 1995 because price incentives will not be sufficient. Gasoline prices in 1973 were such that (in 1973 cars) it cost about 5¢ a mile to operate a 13-mile-a-gallon car. In 1980, it costs 6¢ a mile to operate a 25 mpg car when gasoline costs $1.50 a gallon (in 1980 dollars). In other words, people would be paying only one cent a mile more in their 1980 cars in 1980 than they were in their old 1973 car back in 1973.

"It is not obvious to me that market forces, market forces alone, will push people to go any higher than 25 miles a gallon," said Hippel. Post-1985 standards could thus be required to protect Detroit and provide it with a more stable market outlook.

"Standards could do much better if supported by price incentives. And if we don't have standards, which keep pushing the fuel economy as high as is technologically feasible, at reasonable cost, I think we will have a repetition of what happened in 1973 and 1979. Again and again and again, as our future evolves by a series of crises, rather than by these continuous trends that the scenario writers like to postulate, Detroit will be caught without the cars that Americans suddenly realize they want."

Post-1985 standards, in other words, can protect American automobiles against volatile demand, as motorists respond to short-term changes in gasoline price and availability. It would seem that the standards enacted in 1975 certainly did help American automobile manufacturers in that way, putting them in a better position to cope with the sudden shift in preference in 1979 arising from gas lines and price jumps.

A possible shift in preference and possible rejection of high-efficiency cars constitutes a major concern for an industry contemplating the need to invest tens of billions of dollars to meet standards. The auto makers do not want to be stuck with unsold inventory, which was the case with Detroit's small cars before 1979 and became the case with larger cars in 1979 and after. "The point of standards," observed von Hippel, "is that we have to assure the industry that most people will be willing to buy fuel-efficient cars if they make them."

The problem of adapting to a new oil era poses major challenges for the auto industry. Of late, of course, Detroit's fleet work has been compared — usually unfavorably — to that produced in Japan and Western Europe. But the markets that conditioned those industries have been quite different. "You're comparing, when you say 20 mpg against 28 mpg, an American market against a Japanese market or a West European market," noted one participant. "You're comparing a market that has been habituated to cheap gas with a market where the car designs and the capability of the manufacturers are built on gas at two or three times the American price level.

"We have got a difficult change-over in our industry. Many people say that we have responded too slowly, and perhaps we have. We have some difficulty making enough small cars at the moment. Eventually, we hope to be able to match small car volume against small car demand."

There is considerable uncertainty whether demand will change character again, and, even more important, whether future demand will be interested in the much more efficient cars that *may* be mandated and *could* be built. "The problem," said a participant, "is getting people to buy the cars that go with the gasoline availability and the needed future gasoline consumption."

Other participants expressed the opinion that the auto makers may seriously underestimate future demand for cars that get 35 to 50 miles per gallon and thus fail to prepare for it adequately.

The uncertainty about the market relates directly to an even greater uncertainty — how to finance the investment required to manufacture increasingly efficient vehicles. "The fact of the matter is that Ford and GM compete with cars they build overseas — comparatively cheaply — with other cars made overseas," said Dr. Richard John of the Transportation System Center. "There's little question that technologically a group of American engineers in Detroit could put together a car that people want to buy. The real question is one of economics. Detroit finds itself essentially with a capacity to build 12 to 14 million obsolete V-8 engines and 12 to 14 million obsolete rear wheel drive transmissions. The basic problem is that the American public no longer wants the large car. But the real question is 'Where does the capital come from?' because the only way that Detroit can now raise the capital to build the small cars is to sell the large cars that no one wants."

How much capital is required? In what he described as "a simple exercise," John added up the number of 4 cylinder engine lines, transmission lines, associated components, and so on, that would be involved in achieving a 35 to 40 mpg fleet average by the mid-1990s. "We are talking about a total capital investment of something on the order of a hundred billion dollars." The fuel savings might be two million barrels a day greater than if the standards went no higher than the 1985 target. A similar increase for synthetic fuel plants, which might also produce two million barrels a day by 1995, might also require about 100 billion in capital investment. "So clearly the question whether you go the energy conservation route by building more fuel-economical cars or you tackle the whole issue of building syn-fuel plants is not strictly economic, but really a political economic argument."

And it will shortly become a question to be resolved by the political process. The steps necessary to achieve the 1985 goal are already being taken; the main issue now involves what to do about the post-1985 standards. Legislation to set a 40 mpg standard for 1995 has been introduced by Senators Jackson and Magnuson. "Before there is any such legislation," said James Bruce of the Senate Energy Committee, "some committee, more than one perhaps, will be created and will ask four basic questions. First, what is technically feasible by the mid-1990s? Second, if it is feasible, is it cheaper to build these cars and reduce our oil imports than it is, say, to buy the imported oil or build syn-fuel plants? Or is it in the national interest in some manner to have Detroit build more fuel-efficient cars? The third question is 'can Detroit assemble the capital?' Fourth, if Detroit cannot assemble the capital, should the federal government assist Detroit?"

Some tentative answers, as seen from the perspective of Washington, were offered. "The answers that come back," said Mr. Bruce, "seem to leave no question that 35 to 40 mpg by the mid-1990s is feasible. No question, it's cheaper to do so than to buy imported oil. There's no clear answer regarding the capital requirements." As to the fourth point — "The literature is soft right now; it would be difficult for Congress to make decisions now without additional study."

The central question at the Symposium was rationing vs. gas tax. How can we reshape demand before the next oil shock occurs? Actually, rationing involves a number of different choices and options. Should coupons be transferable? Would the problem of bureaucracy, including the inevitable exceptions, make rationing too cumbersome? Does rationing create a second currency? Would rationing be temporary or permanent? In other words, how manageable would rationing be? The issue was addressed first by John Kenneth Galbraith of Harvard University, who had directed the Office of Price Administration during World War II.

"The choice, of course, is between present levels of gasoline consumption, rationing by the price system, or some direct form of rationing, such as by coupon rationing," said Professor Galbraith. "I am here not to advocate any of those three, but to say a word on the technical problems, my qualification being very largely one of age. I must be the last surviving person who was associated with the last effort at gasoline rationing in World War II, which began actually under my direction as a way of conserving our rubber stocks until the synthetic rubber became available. (We did not use the term 'syn-rubber'. It occurs to me that we were too civilized in those days.) But then when the tankers began going down off the East Coast and the claims of the Air Force for gasoline became very great, gasoline rationing became a necessity.

"At that juncture, the question of rationing was taken out from under my control, and I was confined to price matters, which were sufficient in themselves, but I remained reasonably close to the problem.

"We used coupon rationing based on categories of use. The basic category — A — allowed four gallons for household use a week. There was an intermediate category, and then the highest one, which allowed for virtually whatever was needed. The system was administered by giving coupons to the people in each category, these coupons then being given to the service station on the purchase of the gasoline. From the service station, they were transmitted back to the wholesaler or to the company as the basis for getting the station's next order.

"We also had arrangements with the banks for what was called coupon banking, through which the ultimate accounting was handled. There were various refinements, one of the more interesting of which was coupon weighing — an enormous simplification. We got scales that were fine enough so that within a reasonable margin of error the bank could establish the entitlement of the particular wholesaler or the particular dealer for his next round of gasoline based on the ration stamps he had turned in.

"I think I'm safe in saying that this was not an incredibly difficult operation. Most of the difficulties we encountered were the result of the great insecurity in our supply. I mentioned before one of the reasons — the submarine operations against the tankers off the East Coast. But also we were faced repeatedly with great priority drafts on the oil supplies by the armed forces, and these required very dramatic adjustments. On a number of occasions we had to ban all so-called pleasure driving, simply because we did not have the gasoline to fill the ration requirement.

"There is one very important point I would like to stress. The purpose of rationing is to give the person who has the ration coupon the security that he can go to the pump and get gasoline without waiting. It's an absolute disaster if, when he goes, he finds it's empty. This destroys the entire basis for a successful rationing system, which is security in getting the supply. That was why we sometimes had to ban driving, including in some cases Sunday driving, in order that the rationing coupons could be filled. There was some black market in gasoline. I think we generally had the feeling that rationing gasoline was the hardest thing to do; there was lower compliance in that case than in the case, for example, of food.

"But I think it's also fair to say that, except maybe in Los Angeles, where we had a lot of trouble because of the automobile-based economy, the black market was not an overwhelming question.

"Yet I would be very reluctant on the whole to see that kind of coupon rationing used in the present context. My own thought would be that any rationing system should be very much closer to rationing by price than to the one we used in World War II.

"I would think that the thing to do would be to let the price of gasoline rise and then, tax it up to something close to a penalty level—2, 3, 4 dollars a gallon. Then, using something very closely equivalent to the food stamps, establish maybe two or three categories of rebates that could be used as a substitute for price at the pumps and shift it back through the system. A basic ration of, say, five gallons a week or three gallons a week or whatever, for all household use. And then a somewhat larger ration for anybody who commutes, perhaps some concessions for car pooling. And then maybe a still larger ration for those who use their cars for extensive business purposes, like salesmen or doctors.

"I must say I don't think the administrative problem in handling that would be too severe. There would also be the possibility one could escape the penalty price for an emergency.

"We should allow extra stamps to be given to friends or others if anybody wants to. We didn't allow that during the war because we didn't have the gasoline supplies that permitted it. It was better to keep people from giving away their stamps than to have the much smaller allocation that would have been required if they were allowed to do so.

"Given the situation today, I would let people give away their stamps. Have the coupons expire once a year at Christmas time. People would hold a certain number just for an emergency, thereby saving quite a bit; then the coupons would expire at a time when a great deal of extra driving to use them up wouldn't be possible.

"These are details. My overall thought is that in working out some system of rationing by price that incorporates the ease that is involved with something in the nature of food stamps, one is not committing oneself to an overwhelmingly difficult administrative task. In terms of equity, in terms of political acceptability, there's much to be said for this in a gasoline-based economy as compared with the rather brutal course of letting the price do it all."

Professor Galbraith was echoed by John Bunting, former Chairman of the First Pennsylvania Corporation, who said, "I hesitate to recommend rationing because I think intrusions into our price system should be very few and far between—reserved for a real crisis—a war for instance. And yet I feel that the situation that we have today is a real prolonged crisis and one that does call for a measure such as this.

"I'm distressed that most of my intelligent friends have the same view that there is really no harm—in fact, that there's every good reason for utilizing the fuel that is most available for us—to use the OPEC oil for the next 20 years. What this has done to us in 1974-75 and what it's doing to us in 1979-80 and what it has done to us since 1973 is incredible in terms of the transfer of wealth, transfer of political power, transfer of military power, and transfer of industrial primacy. That will continue to the extent that we continue being dependent on foreign oil.

"So that I come to the question of rationing reluctantly, but I'm persuaded that it's necessary. I go on from there to say it's not going to be easy to bring about. President Roosevelt, not every one's favorite president, but nearly everyone's prototype of what a president should be in terms of being a leader, was not able to get us to arm for World War II in spite of a character like Adolf Hitler running around Europe with Mussolini trailing alongside. It really and truly took Pearl Harbor to bring us into World War II and to really get us to arm. So I don't want to make light of President Carter's problems or any President's problems in bringing us to rationing. It will not be easy. I would even say it would be next to impossible, except that, as I reflect back on events of the past year, I think that President Carter had an opportunity to use the Iranian revolution, and then the occasion when the hostages were seized. I think either of those occasions could have moved us into a system of rationing.

"Now, why not a tax? I have great difficulty there because I kind of like the tax and I like very much Mr. Galbraith's solution. A combination is desirable because it is more consistent with the price system and would be somewhat easier, somewhat more palatable. I think the solution should be something like a $2 tax because I suppose that by the time we get to rationing the price of gasoline will be $2 and we will have, therefore, a $4 price at the pump. And I would suggest that every car would be given 45 coupons per month each worth $2, and we would have a white market in coupons. Banks could even handle it, it wouldn't be too tricky. I certainly agree with Dr. Galbraith. I think the technical implications of this are grossly exaggerated by those who don't like it. And it wouldn't be a difficult thing to administer."

The Symposium turned its attention to standby rationing proposals to be put into effect in an emergency. William Taylor of the Department of Energy said, "What we are doing on contingency planning in general has about four components. One is the strategic petroleum reserve. If we had a great big pool of oil in Louisiana or Texas right now, it would make my job a lot easier. We could sit here more confidently. Unfortunately, we don't have that now. Second, market mechanisms help in an emergency. For example, large import tariffs in the time of an interruption would maintain a lot of the cash flow here in the US rather than flowing to foreign producers. Third, we have government allocations that have had perhaps less than desirable effects. And last, we have rationing.

"There is a distinction to be made between a steady-state rationing plan and an emergency, standby rationing plan. Mr. Bunting, I think, has in mind the kind of long-term steady-state plan to reduce imports, reduce dependence, reduce outflow of dollars. That may be significantly different from what you come up with for an emergency. We are talking about using a rationing plan only when we have a severe emergency. We think it would be very difficult to get any kind of compliance or any kind of an operable system if you don't have some sense of real crisis such as was experienced in World War II.

"For terms of reference, both for talking about gasoline rationing and for talking about alternatives, it may be useful to tell a story about two hypothetical countries—Country C and Country TR—identical in many respects. Individual preferences are the same. Collective preferences may be a little bit different. The two countries consume, produce, and thus import the same volumes of oil. Their imported oil supplies are suddenly interrupted by the same amount. Country C takes the coupon rationing plan that has been described. After a long debate, it was decided to send 10 marketable coupons per week to people who own cars.

"In this interruption, the value of these coupons would rise, let's say, to Mr. Bunting's $2 per coupon; gasoline is controlled at $1.50. So we have a market-clearing price there of the sum of the two figures—$3.50.

"Compare that with country TR, which has great problems with its existing currency, and decides not to set up a new one. Country TR imposes an excise tax per gallon of the same size as the value of a coupon in Country C—$2.00. Instead of sending coupons to everyone who owns a car, country TR sends out a $20 government check to each of those people who own cars. Is there any difference in the outcome between country C and country TR?"

"I have a question for Professor Galbraith on how the decisions would be made on types A, B, or C or how they were made," said David Hunsberger, a Washington consultant. "My understanding is that the Department of Energy at present does not envision interviewing end-users as to what class they think they belong in, but just giving everyone a check or something in the mail. The alternative in which you would actually assign priorities to people in some way suggests there's an interview being made or some lists are kept. I wonder first how that was done in World War II to distinguish A's from B's from C's, and would that be feasible now with 140 million drivers?

"I'm relying on memory here and it's a very deficient instrument after 40 years," replied Mr. Galbraith, "but my basic recollection is that everyone showed up at the so-called War Price and Rationing Board and was given an A coupon. A very much smaller number who needed their cars for professional business or commuting purposes, commuting being very much smaller then, applied for a B coupon. And if my memory serves me, there was a very much smaller number who was allowed to make a C ration claim. So you didn't need to interview everyone; the A coupon was given automatically. However, your point that we have had an inconvenient increase in both automobile numbers and population in the last 40 years is valid. I would accept it."

"I have a feeling that before the day is over we will have thought of lots of pricing substitutes for coupon rationing that we will regard as superior," said Nancy Dorfman of MIT. "I think it ought to be pointed out, though, that Congress has consistently refused in its emergency legislation to permit any form of pricing or taxing as an emergency device. So for the foreseeable future, we seem to be stuck with a rationing plan unless somebody can think of a way of calling a taxing system rationing.

"One thing that bothers me about the proposed rationing plan is how well the coupon market is or is not going to work. I wonder whether the people who will be buying and selling coupons will be in a very good position to know what the value of those coupons is going to be when they want to use them.

"Even the Department of Energy won't know what the gasoline supply is going to be over the lifetime of the coupons, so there will be a problem of getting the coupons to match the gas supply. I can imagine a rather highly speculative market. I don't know which way it might go—whether at the beginning there might be a tendency for people to hold on to coupons, causing the price to go up, or the other way around. But I imagine that people who maybe can't afford to speculate will have difficulty figuring out what those coupons are going to be worth when they really want the gasoline—whether they should buy long or sell short."

"The particular refinements, including the particular price refinements, the details that are so fascinating to members of my profession—these are extremely interesting, extremely important," commented Galbraith. "But I would venture that they are not decisive in the larger question of rationing by coupons as against rationing by price as against using up the renewable resources."

"I believe that according to the most recent modifications of the rationing plan, that DOE will buy and sell coupons to keep the market orderly," said Donald Trilling of the Department of

Transportation. "I assume that this will be somewhat like what a specialist does on the New York Stock Exchange. Some of these features might mitigate part of the problem."

"I think anyone concerned with rationing realizes what matters is what is publicly acceptable," said Clive Jones of Britain's Department of Energy and of the British Embassy. "My experience, especially from our coal strike of 1974, is that any rationing scheme is rough justice unless you want to use half the population in administering it for the other half. What will happen on the basis of our experience in Britain is that in any situation other than clear crisis—clear crises being an oil shortage or war shortage—in any other situation the scheme will start to come apart fairly rapidly as the media focus on the injustices and inequities that undoubtedly will exist in any scheme. This process of media criticism leads to further distortions in the system as the public loses belief in the system, and the system loses credibility. Each individual starts to look for ways of evading it. The whole thing then crumbles.

"For these reasons, rationing as a permanent solution is not at all sensible. As an emergency measure, yes, but in permanent terms for a period of more than six months, I doubt it."

"Unless you have a system that cannot be evaded, one merit of the tax system is that it's less easy to evade taxes than it is some other means of rationing," said Gary DeLoss of the Massachusetts Energy Office.

"Not just evasion," Jones responded, "I might say, but inequities as well."

"If you go with the kind of scheme that Dr. Galbraith was talking about, which can look like a rationing scheme, but has a tax component to it," said Fred Salvucci of MIT, "and if the rationing scheme disappears over time, at least you're left with a tax in place which captures the extra value of the imported oil. From an American point of view it is better to keep that extra value here."

"I want to buttress what Mr. Jones was mentioning about the publicity," said Michael Mosettig of Columbia University, "because during World War II—I have gone through all the periodical literature—there was really remarkably little written about the gas rationing program. I was expecting to go back and find sheaves of articles about people complaining about it, but there are only about six magazine articles during the entire period of war. They just were not wasting their rationed newsprint to complain about the rationing system for gasoline—which just as clearly the media would now, particularly on television news programs."

"If you are going to set a price for these pieces of paper—ration coupons or checks for obtaining them—then there's no reason to distribute anything other than currency," said Gary DeLoss. "In fact, instead of sending out a check that is good for a coupon some time, you send out a check that's good for cash. The real decision is deciding who gets how much. After that, you could construct a partly rebated tax that looks very much like coupon rationing in its equity impacts.

"The second point I'd like to comment on is why so many people have been interested in rationing over the last few years. As a former advocate of coupon rationing, maybe I bear a little bit of the blame. My own thinking has evolved toward the rebatable tax. The average citizen sees a choice between rationing and a high tax, and he resents the high tax option. I think this is why Congress has forbidden consideration of it. The reason they resent it is they don't mind being penalized for excessive use, but they don't want to be penalized for essential use. They think that coupon rationing will protect essential use and penalize excessive use. They think the gasoline tax, by contrast, will penalize essential use as well as excessive use because it applies to every gallon they buy."

"We seem to be closing in on rationing as a short-term emergency measure," said Clark Bullard of the Office of Technology Assessment. "Yet proponents of each of the plans have not addressed themselves to the time required to get such an apparatus under way. I wonder if Professor Galbraith can recall the amount of time it took to institute the World War II rationing."

"My impression is that the gasoline rationing system took another five to six months after rubber," said Professor Galbraith. "There were some dramatic things that had to be done that one could not do now. For example, I believe at one time we requisitioned half the fleet of DC-3's to fly ration stamps out. I think there would be objection to doing that now."

"This is more complicated than giving out food stamps," said Mr. Trilling. "Let me demonstrate some first order complexities which haven't been aired. First of all, if there is a shortfall, you have to design the system to meet public policy considerations. One obvious one would be that we want to do away with discretionary driving to the extent we can, and then ration the rest of the system in a way that impacts the economy the least. This means that you are going to establish a certain base ration for households (which are very difficult to define these days, by the way). And, in addition, you're going to have to establish rations for people who use their cars in business, such as salesmen and car fleets. The next public policy question is how you're going to share the sacrifice to meet the shortfall. This means setting some standards, and millions of people coming to their local rationing boards to apply for their allocations. In one group, there will be farmers and others who will claim absolutely vital needs. In another group, you're going to have Tupperware ladies and Mary Kay ladies, and people who casually use a car in business, yet can demonstrate with tax records how they need a car for business. Clearly, there are a great deal of complexities. Among other problems you're going to have the ration boards playing God with people's ability to earn a living. It gets very, very complicated very, very quickly, much more so than in food stamps."

"Many people have talked about a lot of the administrative problems," said Mr. Salvucci. "I think we learned a lesson in the last decade in this country. It is that we have given virtually no thought to the workability of many of the legislative schemes that we undertake in this country. Gasoline rationing is many orders of magnitude more complex than anything I have ever seen. You are basically talking about creating an entire new currency within a matter of a couple of months. I mean a new currency. You're talking about coupons, you're talking about open market operations, you're talking about checking accounts for coupons. It's got every characteristic of a currency, but reserved for car use. Indeed, it has complexities that the current currency doesn't have, like destroying coupons, keeping track of them through the entire chain from the consumer to the retailer to the wholesaler.

"It's important as one thinks about rationing to think about more than just some theoretical possibilities of equality and equity. One must also consider whether rationing can really work. I don't really know anybody close to the rationing program who thinks it can work."

The other side of the debate is a gas tax, and that is the subject to which the Symposium turned.

"I would like to describe a proposal for a stiff gasoline tax," said Robert Williams of Princeton, "specifically, an increase in the tax to $2 a gallon, with the revenues returned to consumers in two ways. One involves rebating the revenues arising from personal use of gasoline on a per adult basis; the other involves using the revenues generated from business use of gasoline either to offset corporate income taxes or to offset employer contributions to Social Security.

"Why did I choose a number on the order of $2 a gallon? One of the reasons is that many studies suggest that the short-run price elasticity of demand is relatively low, approximately 0.2. With such a low elasticity a tax of this magnitude is needed to get a near-term savings on the order of 10% from the levy of a tax that is rebated. The second reason for doing this is to demonstrate US leadership to the world community in the use of petroleum. A $2 tax is not much higher than present taxes in countries like France and Italy. Finally, a tax of roughly $2 a gallon would leave gasoline expenditures unchanged relative to present levels for those consumers who would shift to cars getting 40-45 mpg, which could be a typical fuel economy for new cars a decade from now.

"There are many ways one can use the tax revenues that are generated from a gasoline tax. My own preference is not to use the gasoline tax as a source of new revenues, but rather to refund the revenues via a tax shift or via a rebate. Congressman John Anderson has suggested returning the tax revenues via a reduction in Social Security taxes. Clark Bullard of the Office of Technology Assessment proposes to rebate the tax to the states and let them decide how the monies should be returned to consumers. Bruce Hannon of the University of Illinois has developed a scheme for rebating the tax so that no income redistribution results.

"While I don't want to argue here that my scheme, involving rebates to adults, is the best, I'd like to point out that it is relatively easy to administer among different options. Also, this particular proposal would address the concern that is most often raised about a gasoline tax—that it would adversely affect the poor. It is often said that a gasoline tax would force poor people out of cars; yet that is not at all what would happen with this particular scheme. This is because poor people (by which I mean the lowest fifth percentile in the income distribution) don't consume much gasoline. Half of the poor don't drive cars, and those that do drive only about half as much as the national average. Thus a tax plan involving rebates distributed equally among adults is fairly progressive.

"The total revenues in the first year resulting from raising the gasoline tax to $2 would be truly enormous—on the order of $150 billion or one-third of the total tax receipts by the federal government in 1979. The rebate per adult arising from gasoline consumed in personal use would be about $700 per year. The extra revenues arising from business use of gasoline could be used either for a 40 percent reduction in corporate income taxes or for a comparable reduction in employer contributions to Social Security.

"One way of looking at the progressive nature of the tax is to ask what levels of gasoline consumption one would expect for different income groups after the tax were implemented. I did a rather crude analysis along these lines based upon income elasticities derived from 1972-73 data and a price elasticity of minus 0.2 for all income groups. Gasoline consumption in the first year might go down about 10 percent. But one would not get a 10% reduction at all income levels. Poor people might actually consume slightly more gasoline than they did before the tax, because their increased income from the rebate would be significantly more than their increased expenditures arising from the tax. Gasoline consumption by upper middle income and well-off people would probably be reduced by more than the average amount—perhaps by 15 to 20 percent.

"How should one go about implementing the tax? It's my view that one should consider two pieces of legislation. The first would be legislation that describes how the revenues would be rebated; the second would establish the level of the tax. It's important to consider doing this in two steps because most people are fairly cynical about taxes. You could say that the proposed tax would not be used as a source of revenues, but people would not believe you. People would have much more confidence in the gasoline tax as a conservation measure if the rebate mechanism were put into place before the actual tax were levied.

"The tax with the rebate is very similar to the proposal put forth by Professor Galbraith as far as its distributional effects are concerned, but it lacks many of the administrative costs of a coupon- or stamp-based system.

"Paradoxically, a stiff tax may be accepted more readily than a modest one. With a fairly modest tax, the benefits are largely social so that one could not expect a strong lobbying effort in support of the tax. But a stiff tax could create a strong constituency of supporters, because as this discussion has shown, such a tax would have considerable private as well as social benefits.

"Probably the most important thing about the gas tax approach is that it would tend to put a lid on the oil 'taxes' already being imposed upon us by OPEC—taxes that cannot be rebated."

"We have been dealing in this session with two distinct problems," said Alvin Alm of the Kennedy School of Government at Harvard. "One is the security problem which, stated simply, is the threat of a supply interruption from which we could have massive economic and personal and even strategic dislocations. Secondly, a long-term economic adjustment problem that's related to our heavy reliance on a dwindling resource in a world where that resource is distributed rather unevenly.

"If you talk about the long-term problem, gasoline rationing makes no sense as a permanent solution for two reasons. One, gasoline rationing is almost pre-emptive self-flagellation. We are inflicting upon ourselves what we are afraid others might inflict upon us. Secondly, and even worse, if you use up a potential emergency tool, such as gasoline rationing, before an emergency, then at the time of emergency your problem is considerably worsened because you will have used up a tool and yet you will have to absorb roughly the same amount of cutback. The reason that that is true is that supplies are allocated internationally on the basis of consumption, so as a permanent measure I would argue gasoline rationing before an emergency is counter-productive.

"Let me move to the security problem. I don't need to tell you how serious is our current vulnerability to supply interruption. The strategic petroleum reserve is the main line defense for the US, and indeed to the extent it helps the price picture, for the world in terms of supply interruption.

"Currently 92 million barrels of oil have been filled in the strategic petroleum reserve, which is equivalent to just five days of US petroleum consumption. Further fill has been terminated since the fall of 1978. Until the US develops a functioning strategic petroleum reserve, we have got only one major alternative that's on the books, and that's gasoline rationing. As an administrative matter, gasoline rationing could in my opinion only work on a permanent basis for which its use will be counter-productive and would not be workable on an emergency basis for which it was designed in the first place!

"That leads me to believe that for the next five to ten years we desperately need to develop alternatives to deal with supply interruptions.

"Now, there are two possibilities. One is some sort of standby authority to institute a gasoline tax with a rebate system to provide the equity features. We have talked about the various ways that could be provided during an emergency.

"The problem with a tax scheme of that kind is how do you know what tax level to use? Will it be effective? Will the tax be too high or too low?

"I'm advocating a system that works much more closely with the marketplace and the current DOE control program information system, namely, thus: During a supply interruption, the President would decontrol gasoline prices. He would collect a windfall profits tax, whatever you want to call it, collect 90 percent of the difference between the base price at the time of the interruption and the market price throughout the course of the interruption.

"This system would work flexibly in allocating supplies. There should be no problem with lines because there will both be incentives to reduce demand, but even more important, incentives for oil companies to move the supplies around in a sensible fashion. And that has been the biggest problem in the last two interruptions—the inability to move supplies around because of the federal allocation program.

"In terms of politics, it is widely thought that taxes are not politically feasible. But, by October 1981, at least in theory, there will no longer be price controls on oil products or on crude oil. At that time, the country basically has two alternatives—either gasoline rationing or complete decontrol with a very massive shift of money going from consumers to producers. What I am suggesting is a tax that would collect that windfall and rebate it to the American people, preventing such a transfer of income. I think under the right conditions, if Congress had to face a proposal such as this compared to gasoline rationing, the probabilities that they would go in this direction would be quite high."

"A question for Bob Williams," said Jonathan Gibson of the Sierra Club. "What would you do in a case where there's an external disruption causing the price to rise? Does your tax remain fixed or is it on a sliding scale so that it would decrease as the price at the pump increased because of world market forces?"

"I have not thought of this as a solution to supply disruption problems," said Williams. "You may very well want to do something along the lines Al Alm is suggesting, to let the tax vary in the event of supply disruptions. I don't think there's any inconsistency."

"I'm wondering if you can overlay Bob Williams' scheme on top of yours," Mr. Gibson said to Mr. Alm.

"Absolutely," Mr. Alm replied.

"What would you do about the fuel efficiency standards?" Mr. Alm asked Williams. "Would you keep them or drop them?"

"I would favor keeping them, in fact increasing them," said Williams. "One of the major problems that we have in energy policy is that we are really in the dark. We can't predict what the outcome is going to be of all our different actions. As far as regulations are concerned, the automobile is probably one of the best candidates for regulation in meeting conservation objectives. What has been demonstrated is that the existence of standards enabled the industry to respond to the present demand for more efficient cars. And there are technological opportunities for much greater improvements in fuel economy. New standards would help the industry adjust to the new oil realities by eliminating much of the uncertainty as to what the long-term demand for small cars is going to be."

"Without the current standards," Yergin said, "it might be argued that Americans would be driving a lot more Toyotas and Datsuns or we would have a real trade war going on now that would have other very serious consequences."

"As the rebate system got into place over time," asked Charles Maier of Duke University, "would people be more likely to view this as an equivalent of their gas consumption—just giving it a different handle—or more likely to see it as an income supplement?"

"If you rebated at the gas pump, then you're not going to have much of an effect," replied Williams. "With my proposal you would have a line on your IRS form that indicates how many adults you have in your household. The rebate would not come at the end of the year, however. There would be adjustments in the withholding rate so as to recycle the revenues back into the economy quickly. In practice, the tax for the poor or maybe for everyone would be pre-bated instead of rebated."

"The question has been raised as to whether you should use

these revenues for transportation subsidies of some kind," he continued. "It is important to realize that, in any case, either most or all of the tax really should be rebated because the revenues are really large—about $150 billion per year with my proposal. Charles Gray, I believe, has thought about how a tax or some fraction of a tax might be used for transportation subsidies; and I wonder if he could make any comments on that, as to the types of things that might receive priority."

"We thought about the need for support to the auto industry for massive change to more fuel-efficient vehicles and some probability of some type of guaranteed loans in particular," replied Charles Gray of the Solar Energy Research Institute Solar/Conservation Study. "In terms of mode-shifting incentives, some very performance-based incentives might be useful. For example, in van pooling initiatives, we should provide a rebate on the basis of how many riders the owner-operator of the van is able to attract—a positive incentive for performance. We think maybe a hundred dollars per rider per year would be enough to encourage a very significant shift.

"In terms of intercity travel, we have come up with a performance-based rebate in terms of passenger miles. As I recall it's about 3/10 of a cent per passenger mile. We are talking about getting 10 percent of the intercity traffic from aircraft and automobiles on the buses, so you're talking about roughly a quarter of a billion dollars per year. With that sort of performance-based incentive, you encourage the bus lines to renovate their facilities and buy new buses and do the positive things to attract more ridership. In terms of subsidy for urban transportation, at least we think that it should be more based on "mass transit." Mass transit subsidies, which are very large right now, should be based again on passenger mile performance of the various urban transportation systems. That kind of stimulus will make them do the right thing, be courteous to the passengers. That's a good example. And those are just examples. We have some more, but in any case there's a lot that can be done with the revenues."

"If you were designing a program, how much a year would you need for a budget?" asked Mr. Williams.

"We also have subsidies with respect to rebuilding the rail industry, 5 to 20 billion over 5 years to essentially just let the railroads catch up with the subsidy that's already been received by the trucking industry," said Mr. Gray. "The trucking industry really pays such a small amount in terms of the deterioration that they cause on the public roads that to have the railroads compete on anything like a fair basis, you'd have at a minimum to bring the railroads back up to the same point in competition. In total, we are talking about a quarter at the most of revenues that you're talking about from such a tax."

"A problem that seems to be associated with any direct rebates is the same as for gasoline rationing," said David Hunsberger. "That's the list of eligible people. This looks like a program where you come up and say 'I'm eligible.' Lists can cause great difficulty in developing either a rationing plan or perhaps tax rebate—the number of people moving, selling cars, getting multiple driver's licenses. Whatever mix you pick, you miss 10, 20, 30 million people or give them an inadvertent double rebate. Have people figured out any reasonable controls to prevent people from signing up with different names and addresses to get a rather substantial extra amount of value? Would we actually be willing at this point to get into a national registry of who we are, which has been very fiercely resisted in the past?"

"Let me talk about a real live rebate program," said Mr. Alm. "When President Carter recommended a crude oil equalization tax, there was a question of what do you do with $14 billion a year in tax revenues. And what was proposed and indeed passed the House of Representatives was a per household rebate for taxpayers. You obviously have registered taxpayers. Your problem is the people who are outside of the tax system. There are two options here. One is a refundable tax credit, for which you have some precedent in the earned income tax credit. Secondly, you can make these funds available through various income transfer programs, aid to dependent children, SSI and other programs. Your problem obviously is those who are nontaxpayers."

"Even if taxpayers had never wanted to file two or three tax forms in the past, they could do so with new Social Security numbers, could they not, and get themselves in the system several times and thus escape?" asked Hunsberger.

"I don't think that's a substantial problem," replied Mr. Alm. "You always have to compare it to what. If you're talking about gasoline rationing, you're talking about trying to get a list of owners of registered vehicles. You have to go to each state. DOE feels that, with about a year to 18 months' work, they could get a good list with which, they say, at optimum they could reach 90 percent of the owners of registered vehicles. Ten percent of the rationing entitlements would be floating around as well as 10 percent of the gasoline."

"I have one comment for each speaker," said Bruce Hannon of the University of Illinois. "Al mentioned that a permanent rationing program would be hobbling our ability to respond to a supply cut-off of some kind or supply reduction or discontinuity. But to balance that, it seems to me you would want to say that a permanent rationing program also reduces the likelihood of a supply discontinuity. It seems it's a question of balancing probabilities.

"To Bob Williams, when you rebate the gasoline tax, you might be able to calculate how much gasoline people would use because of the rebate, but you wouldn't be able to include how much more *total* energy was being demanded because of the rebate. In other words, what's the total impact on the crude oil demands of the rebate?"

"I want to clarify a point," said Richard Michaels of the University of Illinois. "What we are talking about is the use of incentives for modifying the behavior of travelers. Every one of the schemes we have talked about has implicit assumptions about how people will change their behavior in relationship to those policy options. The question at issue is that most of the policy options that we are talking about are what I would call negative incentives or disincentives about using the automobile. The point is, however, that we have not explored the range of possible incentives and the policies for getting changes in behavior in this country at all. And there are a wide variety of both positive as well as negative incentives, local incentives and disincentives as well as national incentives and disincentives."

"It is important to realize the amounts of money we are talking about here," said Samuel Dodson of Exxon. "The $2 a gallon excise tax is $84 a barrel. We are talking about building an economy that is based on gasoline prices that are $84 a barrel higher than the world market. I think we have got to recognize what that does, good, bad, or otherwise. $150 billion a year is about 75 percent of the total personal income tax collections in 1979. So we are not talking about a minor adjustment in fiscal policy of the United States. I might say our company has in fact supported excise taxes primarily across the board for all petroleum products, but on gasoline alone if required, as the most desirable way of moving demand below market levels if that became necessary. But I think we shouldn't fool ourselves about the adjustments in the economy. From a social standpoint, with that much money at stake, people are going to fight very hard for what they are going to get out of it. It is not possible, in large measure, to predict who is going to come out on top."

"Not only do you offer incentives for people to acquire junkers if you run a rebate based on registered vehicles, but you also have an equity issue in that it's mainly the well-to-do people who can afford to buy the extra junkers," said Rusty Schweickart of the California Energy Commission. "You penalize further the lower income segments. Our formal comments to the DOE recommended rebates per licensed driver on the grounds that regardless of your economic status, you can afford a driver's license, so there's less inequity there. Is it because of the potential for fraud that the "per licensed driver" is not a more favored scheme than "per registered vehicle?"

"I don't think either scheme is worth a damn," said Mr. Alm. "But you have literally millions of teenagers and older people who have no intention to drive who would come in to get licenses."

"What number of people are eligible for driver's licenses?" asked Schweickart.

"Substantial," said Alm. "Somebody said thirty million more than currently hold them."

"How does that compare with junkers around?" asked Schweickart.

"It's larger," replied Alm. "There aren't 30 million junkers in workable condition. DOE now rules that a car has got to be in workable condition. I'm not defending this. But I'm telling you the reasons why this was chosen at DOE. Secondly, you have to get these coupons out. Compiling an accurate list on motor vehicles is more feasible than one on licensed operators. Most people suggest rationing coupons on a per capita basis which will be simpler."

"The concept here of asking people like myself to collect $150 billion—and literally that's what you're saying—we have enough problems," said Herb Sostek of Gibbs Petroleum. "I just want you to keep this in mind. We have enough problems with $1.25 a gallon, particularly with the present move to more cash and fewer credit cards. The security aspect of this kind of money floating around in a gas station based on a six million barrel level is substantial, and a lot of money is going to go down the drain. If that isn't bad enough, as that money flows back, I see more government, more bureaucracy, more people, more dissipation. So I don't really think you're going to have $150 billion, and maybe 10 years down the road it will be substantially less."

"Particularly at the federal level in transportation there's a tendency to view transportation almost in isolation," said Mr. Mosettig. "One example right now is that the major proposed budget cuts to bring the budget back into balance involve cutting out a good part of the capital construction money for mass transit. In terms of talking about mass transit in the future, we have to look at the economic development potential of mass transit, particularly if you think how vital transportation is to any economic planning function. With effective mass transportation, particularly if you could make the New York subway safer as regards both the vehicles themselves and crime, it could be a major step in restoring the economic competitiveness of the older eastern cities, particularly as the price of gasoline gets higher in cities where there is no mass transportation.

"I think in terms of selling mass transit, and trying to get money for it. This point needs to be brought out more clearly."

"We ought to underscore the problems of any data base," said John Anderson of the Motor Vehicle Manufacturers Association. "About six states now don't computerize their vehicle registration files. If you do computerize them, most will run months behind because of turnover. Turnover isn't limited just to 10 or 15 million new vehicles sold every year. There are also all the used vehicles. You're talking about a situation where 10 to 15 million vehicles are scrapped every year. There are similar problems with driver's licenses. Some drivers are required to have multiple licenses and multiple registrations depending on the way they operate.

"Unless we go to a system where you go in and sign up and have a control number, a single identified number for every individual, you're not going to be able to get rid of these immense problems and do this on a regular convenient basis. Looking at rationing in an emergency period may be one thing. But on a continuing basis, expecting a 10 percent error is wishful thinking with either of the data bases."

"I believe we have a crude oil problem and not a gasoline problem, and I would want to tax crude oil," said Bruce Hannon of the University of Illinois. "But a tax on crude oil would produce a windfall to coal and perhaps to other fuels that compete with the various components of the crude barrel. So I actually favor a tax on all energy forms across the board. For example, with a gasoline tax, I can imagine people using rebates to put air conditioning into their homes. I'm sure that we really don't want that to happen. So I'm for a tax on all forms of energy (except solar). I think that a tax on all energy forms would promote a renewable energy source development.

"We could collect this tax as energy leaves the ground—a severance tax. The severance tax would then cause conservation of oil and all other forms of energy as well, throughout the whole economic system. It would cause energy conservation in industry, in government, and in the household. A tax on gasoline is also very income-regressive. We would have to be extremely careful about how it was rebated to avoid over-rewarding at any particular income level.

"Another reason for energy severance tax concerns the political susceptibility of the rebate. We must face the possibility that for various political reasons, legislation which started out with a full rebate plan wouldn't make it through Congress. Or, perhaps two or three years later, the rebate would be redirected by additional legislation. If this were the case, I'd rather be left with a tax on primary energy. It's much less regressive than a tax on gasoline.

I'm in favor of the household as the basis for receiving these taxes, mainly because it's so easy to do.

"If we are to use this tax to bring about any significant reduction in our energy dependency, we need to keep the tax rising faster than either wages or interest rates (or both). We want to avoid the sort of phenomena we found after 1974. While there was an immediate energy price increase relative to wages in 1974, during the following years we saw wages catching up with energy prices. Consequently, the idea of conserving became a less important one in most people's minds.

"In our research we have noticed that an energy reduction is associated with an increase in the number of people employed. This is a very important result. If energy prices go up slowly enough, the economy has a chance to adjust and become more labor-intensive. Very sudden shut-offs in the energy flow could, of course, reduce employment.

"The structure of the rebate, how it comes back to us, is very important. Does it come back in the weekly pay check, as a reduction in income tax? Does it come back once a year in a lump sum? These rebate forms will likely be spent in different ways, with different energy-using consequences.

"Finally, I want to bring up one point in favor of rationing. Rationing coupons can represent a store of value. This is a physiocratic point of view, but I can't resist the temptation to bring it up here. Coupons, if they have no time limit, allow consumers to hold energy instead of dollars. That is, they let us hoard energy in a coupon form. This behavior, it seems to me, gets us away from the tragedy of the common behavior which I see going on all the time. At present, for example, we really won't switch off a light or avoid a drive when we know we are just saving energy for someone else. Rationing coupons have the unique effect of presenting us with a chance to store energy. **Further, if the coupons are established on a BTU basis, we can** move them about, buy fuel oil when we want to heat our home a little more and drive a little less, or heat your home a little less and drive a little more."

"I think price, a tax with a rebate is the right way to do it," said George Babikian of ARCO. "My personal opinion is that it's the most equitable way to do it, although there are problems with it. I think the problems connected with tax and rebate are much smaller than problems connected with rationing or some of the other methods. There is indeed an elasticity in gasoline demand—people drive less if it costs more. This elasticity is far greater than we think it is. I don't have absolute data to support that opinion. It's more of a visceral feeling. I do have some facts that confirm it in my own mind and I think they are reasonably accurate. We are having some diminished demand today because of the inconvenience of purchasing gasoline. But fundamentally most of the decrease we are seeing in demand, roughly 10 percent, is due to price. One of our people went back about a year ago and looked at the price of gasoline in real terms. He calculated that in 1959-1960, the average person in this country had to work something like nine and a half minutes to buy a gallon of gasoline. That same person at the end of 1978 had to work six and a half minutes to buy the same gallon of gasoline. It wasn't until the third quarter of 1979 that the number went back up to what it was 20 years ago, about nine and a half minutes per gallon of gasoline. So price really did not act as a rationing mechanism in this country, in my opinion, until the fourth quarter of 1979.

"The latest price in this country, of about $1.25 a gallon, works out to about 11 minutes per gallon. So even with that weak signal, we are beginning to see meaningful conservation and I think it's going to be far greater than any of us are willing to project.

"I looked at some heating oil figures just the other day. We have four fairly large heating oil subsidiaries, one of them right here in Boston. We have about 130,000 heating oil customers. The numbers in each of our big heating oil subsidiaries indicate there's been a reduction of somewhere between 30 to 35 percent, weather-adjusted, in the use of heating oil since the 1973-74 embargo. That's due almost entirely to price. Price has gone up in heating oil about two and a half times since that time.

"So I think price will act as an effective rationing mechanism. I think it can be increased in a way that will result in a two million barrel a day reduction in gasoline demand. Gasoline is the right place to get the decrease, because it's the area where we waste petroleum. And I'm optimistic it will happen."

FLEXIBILITY IN AUTO USE?

Driving patterns have received surprisingly little attention. There has not been a great deal of research on how people use their cars. But the evidence that does exist suggests a much greater flexibility than might have been thought.

"The question today is how do we get significant reductions in the use of the private automobile," said Richard Michaels of the University of Illinois. "And we should recognize going into that question that this is an auto-dominant society. It has developed around the automobile. It is an essential part of the total process by which our society functions today. There is no way that in our suburbanized society we can, over the short run, do without the automobile.

"But when we look at the behavior of the household in particular, there appears to be a major slippage in the way in which people are using the automobile. That is, there is very little organization of travel. We have never had to think about this functionally. At the prices we had to pay for automobiles and for gasoline, there naturally has been a lack of restraint, and so we have never had to do what you might call trip organization and trip planning.

"When you begin to look at this, you discover that there is an enormous wastage in the way we use the automobile. That is true in what we classify as discretionary driving. It involves travel required by the household for medical care, for social purposes, for shopping, and for personal business. These kinds of travel amount to about 75 percent of all the trips made by members of the household. But this travel is generally not organized, hence considerable gasoline is wasted. One of our problems is how to reduce the wastage in discretionary travel.

"There is also considerable wastage in work trip travel. Although we have talked about a lot of alternatives to the automobile, such as mass transit and ridesharing, these can provide only marginal fuel savings. However, the way in which we use the automobile to travel to work has never been considered from an energy efficiency standpoint. People tend to take very restricted routes to work—those which generally have high congestion—hence ones in which the energy efficiency is quite low. These, too, can be modified and offer us a real opportunity for conservation.

"Our best estimates are that in both these domains there is probably an opportunity to save somewhere between 15 and 30 percent of the total gasoline expenditure in household travel.

"How do you get this kind of reduction? This requires behavior change on the part of the traveling public. You are dealing with 60 million households, and 140 million drivers. You have to find ways to modify that at an informal as well as a formal level," Michaels continued.

"This requires at least four things. One is to provide travelers with knowledge on how to use the automobile efficiently. What kind of trip planning will bring about significant reduction in gasoline usage in the automobile? What's the most energy conserving route to use in going from where you are to where you want to go? A second requirement is to devise procedures and methods that individual households can integrate into their own daily lives in terms of the way in which they both view and operate an automobile.

"A third is to provide incentives—both formal and informal. There are social incentives which we use all the time to modify behavior: a car pool is given a preferred parking space; contests for most mpg; public recognition for conservation behavior. I would point out that past experience indicates that these kinds of rewards have been at least as effective as purely economic controls.

"Finally, we need a communications structure that allows us to transmit information to people and to get feedback from them.

"The lack of planning for auto use led and continues to lead to inefficient use of the automobile. There have been recent studies to indicate that this is reversible, which offers positive opportunity for energy conservation. During the 1973 and 1979 shortages, households cut down on their travel mainly by reducing social and recreational trips. Further, recent pilot studies in the New York Department of Transportation on household behavior found that during the 1979 shortages, households were able to curtail up to 20 percent of their non-work travel. These results suggest that experience, knowledge, and real incentives can lead to a significant reduction in auto energy consumption."

"We started out framing a dual problem here of gallons per mile and miles per household," noted Clark Bullard of the Office of Technology Assessment. "A little perspective on the miles per household might be gained by looking from 1950 to the present. Around 1950, the average person spent about 25 minutes per day in an automobile. In the mid-1960s, it reached 40 minutes per day. In the 1970s it saturated at about 60 minutes per day. If we maintain our past 30 years' average speed of about 30 to 35 mph, the implications of the Exxon forecast would be around 80 minutes per person per day in an automobile. Perhaps

Europe responded or adapted to higher prices not by high technology increasing miles per gallon, but by cutting down the miles per household or adopting living patterns that facilitate conservation. Over the last 30 years in this country we have made a massive change in the number of miles per household; we may do well to exploit this flexibility to achieve conservation."

There was a surprisingly strong sense that ridesharing could play a much more significant role than normally assumed.

"The kind of contingency plans around increased use of mass transit, ridesharing, car pooling, van pooling shouldn't necessarily be viewed as alternatives to rationing or taxation," said Fred Salvucci of MIT. "A rationing plan or a taxation plan doesn't really solve the problem of mobility. It simply transfers that problem to individuals in terms of how individuals will choose to use less gasoline. But the problem is still there. People will have to drive less if they're going to consume less gasoline.

"So methods to help people maintain their mobility in the face of reduced gasoline would be necessary complements to a rationing system or a taxation system. You could also try to implement programs to assist people in increased use of ridesharing or public transportation in the absence of increased taxes or a rationing scheme. I think that's wise.

"But you shouldn't view it necessarily as alternatives. There is a problem in trying to put price tags on these various programs in terms of how many dollars you spend per BTU, because an effective program to deal with the energy situation as it has been mapped out here will really require a combination of all of the features that we are talking about. In addition, one is buying different kinds of conservation within different time frames.

"In other words, you can't compare a contingency plan which is designed to consume less energy a month from now if we were hit with a sudden shortfall with a scheme that's designed to have us consume less gasoline 10 or 15 years from now. These programs are really complements to one another in several applications.

"Conservation and contingency planning have to be viewed as two parts of the same process in the petroleum situation we are in now. In other words, you can put out a lot of programs intended to encourage the conservation of gasoline and be very disappointed in the results.

"You can improve public transportation, you can provide ridesharing information, you can put up billboards telling people to drive 55, and not get satisfactory results. If suddenly there's a shortage of petroleum because foreign events shut it off, those conservation initiatives that you had out there that the public didn't much respond to may become very important.

"In fact, if you get hit with a shortage of petroleum and you don't have a lot of conservation schemes out there, you may well find it's too late to introduce any of them because they all take a lot of lead time to put together. The payoff you can expect on transit, paratransit, and ride-sharing strategies is, I think, not of the same order of magnitude as one that you could expect from a rationing scheme. Roughly 45 percent of the gasoline is consumed by 15 percent of the households. Doing some arithmetic and turning that around, you could conserve 30 percent of the gasoline consumed if you rationed everyone at a 70 percent level and only affect 15 percent of the households.

"There is no other conservation initiative that could "save" 30 percent of the gasoline while involving so few American households. You should not view these various programs as competitors; they complement one another. But you should also have a sense of the relative power of the various initiatives. I am not necessarily saying that that's a reason to ration gas. The 15 percent of households doing all that driving may have very good reasons for doing that amount of driving. It's one of the things I don't think we know enough about. But there's at least a potentially significant impact there that I don't think one can anticipate from the more voluntary sort of friendly initiatives that are usually part of the normal conservation initiatives.

"There are four kinds of programs that tend to get talked about within these areas. The first involves measures to maintain order at the gas pump—odd-even, minimum purchase, maximum purchase," Mr. Salvucci continued. "A lot of them are inconsistent with each other. There's also a fair amount of debate as to whether any of them does any good. That's one category. The second category includes measures to increase the gasoline efficiency of the vehicle miles traveled. Basically those are initiatives to reduce speed. The principal focus has been on driving at 55. As a rule of thumb for any speed higher than 42 miles an hour or so, you tend to save about 1 percent for every mile per hour you go slower.

"The tuning up of the automobile, maintaining correct—or even a little higher—pressure in your tires: that sort of thing also has a reasonable payoff. About 10 percent savings is potentially available there. Not that any one initiative is able to squeeze it out, but I think it's useful to identify that pool of gasoline as one that is probably most easily available at least cost to the rest of the economy and recognize that no one initiative will get at that whole amount.

"A third category of steps that are particularly interesting consists of measures to increase the number of person miles traveled per vehicle miles traveled. That's basically trying to get people to walk more, to take public transportation, to car pool, to use vans, etc.

"And the main target in those kinds of activities is, I think, appropriately, the journey to work. Roughly 34 percent of vehicle miles traveled is in the journey to work. It is one of the least efficient trips by automobile. Car occupancy on the journey to work is down somewhere between 1.2 and 1.4 persons per car, whereas for other sorts of travel the car occupancy is much higher. So it is a useful trip to target for several reasons. It is done in a relatively inefficient way. It is done every day with a great deal of repetition. And you have people grouped at least at one end of the trip at an institution that has some influence on their lives, namely the employer. Roughly half of American employment occurs at places of employment of a hundred or more employees. So you've got an institution which presumably has some sophistication, some ability to deal with something complicated, involved with about half of the work trips in the country.

"So that seems like an appropriate place to target. And probably the employer as an institution getting involved in trying to encourage employees to travel in more fuel-efficient ways is one of the more significant new initiatives we can make use of. The employer has a stake in fuel conservation and is in a situation to encourage people to make the journey to work in a much more fuel-efficient manner. This is, I think, the best opportunity that we are looking at which has not been explored.

"Reduced gasoline consumption through increased use of transit, paratransit, and ridesharing, in particular through improved efficiency of the journey to work, is nearly as painless as the vehicle efficiency strategies. This will require expenditures for transit, and very aggressive participation by employers to achieve significant results. In addition, there may be a dampening effect on imported small car demand. These problems are more than offset by the private savings, reduced petroleum imports, avoidance of significant mobility impairment and the consequent economic dislocations, and reduced congestion and air pollution.

"We have in place a whole set of transportation planning units all over the country which are largely composed of public officials. There are state highway departments, there are cities, there are transit authorities, etc.

"That whole network of people has tended in the past to be preoccupied mainly with increases in infrastructure—to build another highway or don't build the highway. The people involved are either construction interests who want to build the road or environmental interests who want to prevent the road from getting built. But rarely are they people who are primarily concerned with mobility.

"So the whole existing network of institutions is not aimed at getting more efficient travel accomplished. Car pooling, which probably has the greatest potential in a very short time for changing the amount of gasoline consumed for a certain amount of transportation, is now entrusted usually to the highway department. The highway department in most states has a vested interest in something like car pooling not working because the highway department's funds come at so many pennies to the gallon of gasoline. And the rewards of being a good highway administrator result from getting more highways built, not getting more people into car pooling. The current set of institutions that have responsibility in this area, particularly car pooling and van pooling, which are some of the more significant quick turn-around devices, don't have a major interest in the job that they have been given."

"The question that occurs to me is whether anybody has looked at putting money—whether it's raised by gasoline tax or any other way—into some form of subsidization or incentives for some of these alternatives, mass transit being one of the most obvious," said Mr. Benjamin of the Associated Press. "I don't think its necessarily frivolous to talk of the possibility of providing an easier incentive to people to use bicycles and motor bikes and motorcycles to get to work—one of the serious problems in this country being safety. What about something as simple and relatively low-cost as dedicating traffic lanes, or even reserving entire streets, which don't have to be very large streets, as commuting streets into town strictly for two-wheeled vehicles, let's say, except for residents who have to park on the street or something of that sort? So I wonder whether we have any thought on the positive incentives for alternative forms of transportation since that is what we are really talking about."

"The rational impact of a lot of the incentives you may think of may be much less significant than the sort of nonrational or symbolic kind of value," replied Mr. Salvucci. "For instance, recently in Massachusetts, the Turnpike Authority, which runs a toll road, raised their tolls and put in a toll structure that allowed car pools to ride for slightly less money on the toll. If you have three people in a car instead of one and the toll was, let's say, 60 cents, you already had it down to 20 cents per person. If you lower that toll, you may have those people riding for 19 cents apiece instead of 20 cents apiece, or even 15 cents apiece instead of 20 cents apiece. That nickel isn't going to change anyone's behavior pattern by any analysis you make about what one should do for a nickel a trip. But what you are doing with that kind of incentive is taking an activity which is probably rational anyway and sort of blessing it, making it acceptable, giving the signal that the society is encouraging you to do this.

"I remember World War II, but not too well," he continued. "I suspect that victory gardens made a lot of sense for people if they wanted to have some decent vegetables. But gardening was a sort of low-class form of activity. That's what the immigrants and people in from the farms did. Nice people grew hollyhocks and not tomatoes. But saying it's patriotic to have a victory garden allowed lots and lots of people to grow vegetables for whom it made sense to grow vegetables.

"It makes a lot of sense to car pool. It makes a lot of sense to take mass transit or take a bike, but in the past it's not been viewed as a status kind of activity. So when the employer takes the reserved parking spaces that were always reserved for the big shots and says that the people who car pool get to use those parking spaces and the president of the company has to walk 20 feet or 50 feet, you're providing an important symbolic gesture. I don't know how you predict how well those things are going to work. You just try them.

"A second area involves a slightly longer-range look. Even at higher gasoline prices, with a more efficient car it's going to cost you only 6 cents a mile for gas to run your car. Once you own your car and pay for the insurance, economic incentives are not going to get you out of that car very easily. On the other hand, if it's very easy to car pool or take public transportation and you conclude that you can get by with one less automobile in the family, then you've got a real incentive facing you. If a three-car family decides to become a two-car family, there's probably a pretty big incentive for that. A pretty large number of people are making those decisions every year. Play with that arithmetic and figure out the rate at which vehicles get scrapped and sold off into the used car market. Roughly one out of every three households is making a decision to dispose of an automobile every year. That's a very large target population which could, in the right environment, accelerate these decisions. Roughly one out of three households is moving every year. Again, with energy as a priority and with a lot of public information on different ways of getting to work, people could move in order to live closer to where they work.

"Finally, operating subsidies for public transportation are seen as an incentive to encourage people to ride public transportation. I think that's an inaccurate view. In point of fact, the operating subsidies for public transportation systems are a *necessity* if you want to have those public transportation systems at all.

"The transit providers are under intense pressure from inflation. Most transit workers have automatic cost of living provisions in their contracts. So it is very difficult for your transit authority to give you as much service this year as it gave you last year. And by and large they are already providing the transit system in the natural market. If you're talking about extending that service, you're talking about going into lower density areas. I am a strong advocate of public transit subsidies and I think they ought to be bigger, but I don't think they ought to be viewed as a simple incentive to abandon automobile travel that's automatically going to get a response. You need these subsidies if you're going to have public transit around at all. But don't think that because you spend a little more money in that category you're going to see a shift in behavior."

"Two years ago, of people who used vehicles to get to work, about 21 percent shared rides," said Donald Trilling of the Department of Transportation. "If you wanted to increase that by 5 percent, it would only involve a shift into ridesharing of about one percent of all commuters. That didn't sound like much. But when you look at the composition of the people who shared rides, we have some data that indicate that some 60 odd percent of them come from the same family. In other words, they are husband-wife combinations or father-daughter combinations or such. This means that you are really trying to obtain the whole increase from the remaining 40 percent of the ridesharing base. Recognizing that, it is apparent that a 5 percent increase will mean quite a shift in people's habits to get them to convert to ridesharing. We ought to be aware that it may be more difficult than most people would think at first blush."

The Symposium sought to find a balance between the various choices within the larger political context—starting with the difficult issues of equity.

"In most discussions of equity and gasoline consumption, in a group as large as this one," said Professor Thomas Schelling of Harvard University, "the first equity issue that comes up—and sometimes the only one—is whether even in principle the price system might be used to induce conservation, to allocate gasoline to where it is most needed, or to provide incentives for new technology and new production. I have rarely been in a group this large where one could talk about using the price system to ration energy, any kind of energy, without being jumped on by people who take for granted that market pricing and equity are not compatible.

"But I think there is progress, and the sign of it is that until recently rationing didn't mean what it means here today. Only recently has rationing been thought of in terms of marketable coupons. To my generation, selling ration coupons was a contradiction: rationing *meant* not using the market.

"But people are becoming familiar with the proposition that, however good or bad fixed-quota rations are, marketable rations are probably better, even for the poor—or especially for the poor. Some of them are beginning to learn that if you can like marketable rations, there's usually some alternative you can like even better.

"I just wish we could stop using the euphemism 'white market,' and recognize that the word 'market' means eactly that. We don't need to give it a color, especially the colorless color, white.

"Once we agree on trying to use the price system to allocate a reduced quantity of gasoline among consumers, the first equity problem that arises is how to capture the windfalls," Professor Schelling continued. "What we are discovering is that there are innumerable ways to do it. We can do it at the level of crude oil, the gas pump, or marketable coupons. What we are talking about is how to keep all or a large fraction of a price increase—the part that doesn't perforce go to foreigners over whom we have no control—from going to oil companies, land owners in oil territory, lucky bidders on offshore leases, service station owners, and so forth. Much of the proceeds go back into the tax system through corporate profit taxes and personal income taxes; but there is a strong desire to capture even more of it. And whether we do it with marketable coupon systems or crude oil windfall taxes or incremental excise taxes on gasoline, these are all alternative ways of keeping higher prices from redistributing sizable amounts of income to the people concerned with oil.

"The poor consume so little of the gasoline that we ought not to try to design market systems or coupon systems or tax systems primarily to take care of the poor. The poor should be taken care of through programs focused on poverty; the details of these gasoline schemes should be designed for the rest of us who consume most of the gasoline.

"The first order of business, whether or not we like marketable coupons or taxes or any other sort of market system, is to find a way to take care of the poor, either the poor who are made especially poor by rising energy prices or just those who are poor whatever happens to the price of gasoline. Only if we do that can we free ourselves from the awkwardness of having our whole approach to gasoline determined by the impact that our gasoline program will have on the people who, precisely because they are poor, as well as because often they are elderly, consume only a fifteenth or a twentieth of it.

"Once we settle that issue, we move on to all of those rationing details that relate to whether my son drives a low-mileage pickup truck, or you make your living by driving to work in the outskirts, or one of us has handicapped children to drive to school, or one of us makes a living by driving from house to house. Am I to be rewarded with a larger ration for having a gas guzzler, or penalized even if I can't afford a new car? Most of the discussion is about how most of us are going to end up paying more for the gasoline we burn and getting most of the difference back one way or another.

"And what we have all discovered is that there's a multitude of newly equivalent ways to do it. They differ in detail, in how they discriminate among the rural and the urban, the self-employed and the factory-employed, the elderly and the younger, the people who live three in a family and the people who live alone. But, for the most part, the difference between the worst system and the best system in terms of the amount of money involved is of no great magnitude. Especially if the coupons are marketable, the difference between the right rationing system and the wrong one will not be an absolute limit on essential driving for somebody who needs more coupons than he gets. It will be equivalent to a higher price of gasoline.

"There are three things to say about a coupon system," Mr. Schelling went on. "First, it is absolutely essential that the coupons be marketable. All of those terrible details that seem almost unmanageable in determining who should get how big an allowance involve only limited damage as long as the worst that happens is that you are going to pay more for the gas you use when your ration was not enough. Second, as I've already emphasized, the system should not be designed for the poor. The poor should be taken care of some other way. And the third point is that any coupon system, even a marketable system, should be explicitly temporary, with a firm expectation of being phased out soon.

"The reason is simple. The whole point of marketable coupons is to make the marginal cost of gasoline equal to the sum of the pump price and the coupon price. And it will not be, if the way you qualify for next year's coupons is to drive long distances this year. If you get a larger ration on account of living out in the country or having a job that requires you to do a lot of driving, and you'll only continue to get a big ration if you continue to stay in the country and do that job that requires all that driving, then a lot of the adaptation to higher gasoline prices that we want people to begin to do now for the long run they will not do because they will lose their rations. Like a government agency that is afraid to save money for fear its budget will be cut the following year, people who respond to the higher price of gasoline by making alternative transportation arrangements that do not require as much driving will be in danger of losing whatever special treatment they get under the ration system.

"So any system that discriminates according to need, by tending to reward continued need, will tend to preserve some of the legacy of the low-price driving patterns of earlier years. And since the only reason for using coupons instead of taxes is to discriminate in favor of people whose living and working patterns, reflecting the low gasoline prices of earlier years, require them to burn lots of gasoline, we won't get all the benefits of the market system unless we phase out the rationing element.

"Three things are crucially important for the economy and I think are technically manageable," Mr. Schelling continued. "One is the Consumer Price Index. It should be recognized that this is a legal entity. It has statutory and contractual existence. It is the official number to which many things are indexed. We should keep in mind that the CPI does not include in its market

basket anything called coupons; and the CPI does not distinguish between marginal prices and average prices. There may be
a legislative decision to make—whether to include the coupon
price along with the pump price in the CPI, or to recognize that
the average price of gasoline is merely the pump price if the
coupons are treated as a transfer system among consumers that
cancels out. Alternatively, if the cash value of the coupons is
treated as a cost of living subsidy, it can offset the coupon price
of gasoline. Similarly, if there's a gasoline tax coupled with a
rebate system, it may be possible to use the rebate in a way that
offsets the nominal increase in the price of gasoline, either by
treating the rebate as a cost-of-living subsidy in the CPI itself, or,
as some have proposed, to effectuate most of the rebate by
lowering other taxes that are included in the CPI. This is all
manipulative, but it is important. Retirement benefits by statute,
wages by contract, are legally attached to the CPI. It is not merely
a statistic; it is a legal entity.

"Second is the question what it all looks like to OPEC. Some
people think that a tax makes the nominal price of gasoline go
up and OPEC will feel invited to raise its price, while with
rationing the pump price will stay low and the coupon system
cancel out. Maybe what's going on can be camouflaged with a
coupon system. Maybe OPEC would pay more attention to an
import fee on crude oil than to an excise tax on gasoline. All of
this may matter, but I doubt that it matters much. Since I am
unsure whether it makes a difference to OPEC and if so, what it is
that makes the difference, I would let my decision be determined by what works best domestically, but I admit I may be
wrong about that.

"Third, in the event that we use a tax with some kind of rebate
system, not a coupon system, there will be good macroeconomic
reasons for recycling rapidly. And I do not see why that needs to
be difficult.

"Most of the discussion has been about rationing or taxation
to induce conservation, but what is more important is to have a
system ready for a serious emergency, an unexpected need
quickly to restrict gasoline consumption," Mr. Schelling
stressed. "While we are spending months or years discussing
what kind of sophisticated marketable ration system or tax-
rebate system we would prefer, events may overtake us. If something happens to interfere severely with Persian Gulf exports we
have about two months during which the tankers that have
already left there are still on the way. But two months is a very
short time to put a rationing system into effect, and not much

time to perfect a tax-rebate scheme. The most important thing will be to have some system either in place or ready to go promptly to cope with such an emergency. Very likely in an emergency the one thing that can be done quickly is to use the President's authority to put a fee on crude oil imports. He can put a tax on all crude oil by putting twice that tax on imports and going back to the old entitlements system to average it over all the crude oil purchased by refineries. And if he has in place a windfall excise tax, that will take care of some of the domestic windfall. He will need a faster way to recycle the proceeds than he has now.

"There is still the question, do you really want to use the price system in an emergency? This is where the differences among us may become pretty great. A lot of people think that it's easy to use the price system in the smooth long run when everybody gets a chance to adjust and nobody's taken by surprise. But if the Strait of Hormuz were blockaded and we face an unexpected severe shortage, then do you believe in the price system?

"My answer is yes. In fact, that is when it really matters. It is precisely when you're dealing with severe shortages, when you're down to the genuinely inelastic demand—that is when misallocating the liquid fuel is something we cannot afford. That is precisely the time when people who cannot do without gasoline have got to be able to get it by paying for it. Don't say that if they are too poor they can't do it; if they are too poor, they weren't going to get it anyhow. And even the poor will sometimes need gas so badly they would rather pay an exorbitant price than be protected from the high price by being forced to do without. It is precisely when the emergency hits and the price of gasoline may go up by amounts measured in dollars rather than quarters, when the tax proceeds may be $150 billion rather than $50 billion annually, that we had better be ready to go ahead with a flexible tax scheme. The alternative is chaos and inequities that cannot be measured in the price of gasoline."

Of course, what is practical may not be doable. The experience of what is now going on for seven years suggests that interests and perceptions tend to be so much in conflict and so confused that consensus building and decision making in the political realm where the choices are adjudicated can be slow and painful processes. There seems to be a very deep and widespread presumption in the United States that gasoline is to be cheap and easily available. Any other condition is the result of some plot. Moreover, the necessity to fill up often means that gasoline price and availability is perhaps the single most vivid direct contact that most Americans have with the energy problem. Naturally enough, elected representatives are very alert to what they perceive as their constituents' sensitivities on this point.

Thus, inevitably, the Symposium turned its attention to implementation—what to do—and what can be done—in the American political process.

"The acceptability of rationing by purse was mentioned earlier," said Professor Ted Marmor of Yale University. "The question I have about that is, to whom is that acceptable now? Is it acceptable now to this group, acceptable to a set of elite publics? How wide is that acceptability? Mr. Schneider's paper suggests that rationing by purse has its critics. I don't want to say they should be determinant, but I think it is important to worry about the education process and the nature of that opposition.

"It strikes me that the difficulties that are identified today reveal over the last five years something close to an institutional crisis or at least an extraordinary stalemate—in coping with external threats and the interruption of supply, an internal incapacity to coordinate action against those threats of interruption of supply. We have a congressional and presidential stalemate on how to cope with an extraordinary social malaise. One has to worry about the viability of such a political order.

"I took very seriously the point in the Schelling paper that there are certain versions of taxation plus rebates that look very close to certain versions of rationing. If the political meaning of various combinations varies more than the substantive allocational effects, it behooves us to spend a lot of time thinking about the various versions.

"With the tax plus rebate plan, it seems to me crucial not to ask about its implementation if it were accepted, but to ask to what degree you could implement that joint choice. Could the rebate come first, and tax second?

"That's quite different from the objections that can be raised about the rationing. The problem with respect to implementing rationing is not getting political support for it, but *doing it*, with the rough justice in the short term and horribly rough justice, or so it appears, over the longer term.

"Thus, the problem of implementation looks quite different when you look at the tax plus rebate scheme than when you look at the rationing one. The realistic comparison between the various combinations, it seems to me, would be highly attentive to reasonable forecasts of implementation under both those headings."

"We have to look at this problem in two categories—in terms

of an emergency which is a chronic emergency and one which occasionally becomes acute," argued Ben Cooper of the Senate Committee on Energy and Natural Resources. "The acute emergency is the situation which I find more interesting and also much more scary. Our policy in that regard is to have a strategic petroleum reserve and I don't understand why we are not putting more oil in it than we are now. The rest of the system that we have, which is all we have now, is standby gasoline rationing.

"You can argue whatever you want about whether these systems work or not. On the one hand you can have a white market rationing system with a market-determined value for the transferable coupons. On the other hand, you can have a tax equal to the value of the market price of the white-market coupon. These two don't look a whole lot different if we take the proceeds of that tax, put it in the same envelope, in the same numbers as we were going to use for the coupons, and send it to exactly the same people.

"I think you can argue you wouldn't like the tax-based system, but you can't argue it's less equitable than rationing with the white market. So I think that as that sort of becomes obvious to the body politic, we may have a chance to change the way we do it. Of course, the only benefit of explicitly recognizing that what we have is a tax arrangement is we don't have to keep track of these damn coupons. Just give money out and have the money come in. We will save a lot of trouble that way. We won't save all the trouble because we will still have the massive lists of envelopes to type up and the rules as to who gets more money in their envelope than other people.

"But to my mind the largest energy issue lying around right now is the question of the exercise of emergency authority by the President during the recurring acute emergencies which are going to crop up. That is the issue of the 97th Congress because the only authority available for that now—the Energy Petroleum Allocation Act of 1973—expires in the middle of that Congress. It's academic to talk about rationing gasoline right now because it's going to take 20 months to get the plan implemented and the authority for the President to do it will have expired by then. So it's an issue which we are going to take up. We will take it up next year.

"That brings me back to chronic emergency. It's important to do the right things to improve the situation with respect to our oil imports, because it may make the acute emergency a little easier to live with.

"The secret agenda here at this conference really is whether we are going to adopt a policy of taxing gasoline to deal with the chronic emergency. It's clear and obvious that it will be politically unacceptable to try rationing to deal with the chronic emergency. Centrifugal forces would just drive the system to smithereens, as well as anyone connected with it.

"I think also a big tax is out, too, for a lot of the reasons which have been enumerated. The Finance Committee in the Senate and the House Ways and Means Committee are very peculiar committees in Congress. They are singled out in the Constitution for special treatment because of their revenue raising abilities. And I think that the tactical problems of enacting a large tax probably overwhelm the analytical work that we might do to show what a good idea it is.

"Also, one of the things that you really run up against is that the political system has a way of picking out different problems from those you'd like it to pick out. For example, I think it's difficult to convince Congressmen that you cure inflation by raising prices through taxation. Inflation is the thing that a lot of them see as the problem. The public also has sort of an aversion to abstractions, and I think many members of the public are unwilling to pay $2 a gallon for gasoline for what they may regard as a rather abstract notion—that you somewhat reduce our dependence on some people who are already going to give us trouble anyway.

"We don't want to really confuse means and ends here. The end of public policy is not to get our import rate down, but to keep the system running and make progress slowly and carefully so that we are still sure that young couples can get married and buy a house and have a car and a job and do all the things they think they'd like to do. That's really what we are trying to do. It's important that we keep sight of that.

"One of the other reasons it's tough for us to enact these taxes is that I don't think the political system and the public really believe you when you say that somehow all this money is going to come back and it's all going to be the same after we have raised US energy prices $84 a barrel above the world price and moved $150 billion around within our own economy. It may be true. I profess to be undogmatic about it. But I must say I don't believe it either.

"This fundamental outlook is extremely dismal. That's what it comes down to. All forecasts I know about, including the adoption of what I regard as some fairly ambitious proposals here, would still leave us pretty dependent and in the middle of the same problem we are worrying about right now, and what's more, would leave our allies in the same relative position, only much more dependent. I don't see a way out of it. I really don't."

The difficulties this problem poses for the political process were underlined by David Schooler of the Staff of the House Subcommittee on Energy and Power.

"Obviously, the first hurdle is determining what is the magnitude of the problem, and is the solution any better than the problem itself," said Mr. Schooler. "When the DOE decided they would have a conservation plan, one of the three they came up with was restricting weekend sales of gasoline. By the end of the debate, many people were convinced that that was the problem during our shortage, not the solution.

"The same problem may arise when people ask how are we curing inflation by raising prices.

"One of the unfortunate elements in the continuing discussion over gasoline rationing is that in one sense the Congress has become almost too educated on the issue of income transfers. Both Mr. Galbraith and Mr. Schelling have mentioned in one way or another that the refinements are not all that important. Mr. Schelling notes, I think perhaps correctly, that no matter how you work out your rebate scheme, it probably won't be all that different. Unfortunately, I would say that 90 percent of the Congressional debate has centered around the exact mechanism for giving out the coupons, not whether rationing would work and not its economic implications in a broad sense.

"Prior to that, we began with the crude equalization tax. The House of Representatives was willing to buy a per household rebate. By the time rationing came along, the Senate woke up at least to the fact that there was a massive income redistribution effect from state to state, or at least perceived income redistribution from state to state. By the time they resolved that through an amendment, the House had recognized that the differences among congressional districts within a state are probably worse. And thus we started hearing about suburban versus urban as the issue.

"This suggests to me that the concept of any gasoline tax with a rebate faces the problem of more debate over the rebate than over the tax itself. It may well result, if there is ever to be a gasoline tax, in the use of funds going for some other purpose— not for a rebate.

"Then, of course, we have other problems. Clark Bullard suggests giving it to the states and letting them be the decision makers. But, unfortunately, in the Congress they don't like to be the taxers and let the governors be the good guys.

"With regard to constituencies, I've heard a lot about the fact that this isn't an issue of the poor and thus there should be support because it won't be perceived as hurting the poor. That, of course, is the exact reason why these programs have problems. These programs that would increase the price of gasoline affect the middle class, those who vote, and they affect them in such a differing way depending on how far these people have to drive and where they are located, that there is probably no way of being able to single these people out. But they are the ones who will yell and scream. Congress relates to anecdotes. They relate to letters from people who can write descriptively, or they use their own experience, but it's a question of anecdotes rather than class distinctions. And complainers clearly were the constituency during the last rationing program.

"During the entire time, for example, before the state adjustment factor was put into play, I didn't hear one winning state yelling on behalf of the rationing plan because they would be winners. But on the other hand, states at the bottom were the ones who were yelling because they were losers. I didn't hear, for example, of people with three cars or more telling us to hurry up and implement the plan. Yet we heard many people who have just one car in the entire family telling us that the plan was unfair.

"To give some sort of a positive ending, there is hope in the fact that the Congress has continually called for the development of a rationing plan despite its many rejections of what has taken place. It is notable to recognize that the government at least is looking at rationing plans which could, for example, be the first step towards a tax rebate mechanism. Slowly but surely some people are recognizing the difficulties in implementing rationing and are getting to some degree won over to the concept of the use of a tax rebate mechanism.

"To the extent that we can continue the push and planning in this area, we are not totally behind the eight ball. When that emergency comes, which everyone seems here to be expecting, perhaps that will be enough to turn the tide and we will have done at least the first step of planning which will help tremendously."

The basic question of public attitudes was addressed by Professor William Schneider of the Hoover Institution and the Council on Foreign Relations. "We seem to have reached a vague consensus that there is something more efficient, more desirable, about price rationing than other rationing mechanisms," he said. "The question is whether the public agrees. If you simply look at polls, the public does not.

"I think the basic problem as far as public thinking is concerned looks like this: there is an enormous sensitivity on the part of the American public to price. This shows up in any poll you take on any subject. I want to correct one piece of misinformation. As far as the public is concerned, the energy crisis is not the most important problem facing the country right now. It hasn't really ever been. The most important problem is inflation. Any energy solution that involves any direct increase in the price of energy, in the price of anything, is rejected out of hand.

"The implication of this is that a price rise, a rise in the cost of energy, is likely to involve a heavy political cost. Politicians in Washington are not unaware of what happened to Joe Clark in Canada—who went into the wilderness quite rapidly after having suggested something that would raise the cost of energy. This, of course, is an election year and elections, as Samuel Johnson would have said, like the prospect of being hanged, concentrate the mind wonderfully.

"A recent study I didn't cite in my paper was done by Survey Research Center. They tried to explore the public's actual behavior with respect to fuel consumption. They found that, try as they would, they could not relate driving habits and fuel consumption to people's attitudes about conservation. The degree to which people agreed with the statement that energy resources are limited had nothing to do with people's actual behavior insofar as their use of fuel was concerned. When the SRC explored what factors lay behind the decrease in the use of fuel, the actual conservation of energy, they found overwhelmingly it was sensitivity to cost. This was volunteered when people were asked why they had cut their driving. It was volunteered over and over again.

"So we have this puzzling situation in which everyone rejects any solution that involves raising prices. Yet, on the other hand, that is manifestly the only way to get serious efforts at conservation.

"I should point out another couple of things involved in these kinds of polls. The Survey Research Center also asked people how they thought gas savings should be realized, and they were given several options. One of them was down-sizing cars, another of them was having fewer options, and the third choice was less powerful engines. They overwhelmingly chose less powerful engines in preference to smaller cars or fewer options. The reason for that, which they volunteered quite readily, is the fact that hasn't been brought up at all today—safety. That was the dominant reason people suggested they didn't want to drive small cars. It's a very strong public concern and the most important reason why people don't want to buy smaller cars. Less powerful cars are all right.

"Having cited these conditions in the data and the reason why politicians have to pay attention to them, let me say why, as a longtime analyst of public opinion trends, I don't entirely believe them.

"The consensus in Washington seems to be, among those who read polls and those who don't, and among those who listen to letters and complaints from their constituents, that rationing is the most politically palatable answer. This is being recognized in Washington.

"Let me try to characterize how people respond to the notion of rationing. There are two answers to that question. In any poll I have seen where people are asked whether they approve or disapprove of rationing, coupon rationing of some sort, or permanent rationing, they don't particularly like the idea. The only exception is if it is specifically described as standby rationing in an emergency, which the public generally does approve of. Rationing is approved when and only when it is presented as an alternative to price increases. That's a very important consideration. The general sense that rationing is somehow popular is not entirely true. It's popular only because it's seen as less undesirable than higher prices.

"There is something else to consider with respect to rationing. This also hasn't been brought up today, namely the sources of resistance. People don't particularly like rationing not simply because they want to drive cars as a matter of convenience. I think there is a larger issue involved here than those we have been discussing, and that is freedom. One of the principal reasons why it is very hard to pry people's hands off the steering wheel and get them to car pool and take mass transportation is that the automobile in this country has made a net contribution to people's sense of individual freedom. You can leave for work when you want, you come back from work when you want, you don't have to depend on other peoples' schedules, you can go where you want and organize your life better. Under rationing it becomes somewhat less convenient to do that. There's an important consideration here that would certainly apply to any rationing plan that might be implemented.

"I'd call your attention to an investigation I did some time ago on a very puzzling question. Economists have long suggested, as common sense would suggest, that an income tax is somehow more progressive than a sales tax. But the public always says in response to polls that an income tax is less fair than a sales tax. I always wondered why this was true. So I conducted a little investigation and I found that people have a simple and obvious answer to that question. They say that an income tax is coercive. You have to pay it, you have no choice, they are going to tax your income. But a sales tax isn't. If you don't want to pay the sales tax, don't buy the refrigerator or don't buy a new pair of shoes. In some perhaps misguided perception on the part of the public, they perceive the sales tax as being a matter of choice, as being something that isn't coercive.

"I think very much the same thing would come into play with the alternative between price rationing and coupon rationing we talked about today. A price rationing system, however high, would not necessarily be seen as a coercive system in the same sense that a coupon rationing system would be.

Someone brought up a very interesting distinction—that prices and taxes penalize essential use, while physical rationing penalizes excessive use. The problem is this: who defines what is essential use and for whom is that definition intended.

"It seems to me the definition of essential use and rationing could probably work only in a situation of a real crisis. World War II was a suitable crisis that convinced people to suffer a serious impingement upon their sense of personal freedom. Embargoes, such as that which took place in 1973-74, might convince people to accept significant limitations to their freedom. No evidence I have seen suggests they will do so in the case of a malaise.

"My conclusion generally is something like this: we will probably have to experience coupon rationing in order to have general public acceptance of price rationing in this country. Let me give you one little piece of evidence that suggests that.

"The best question on the whole issue was asked by Cambridge Survey Research in February of 1979, before the gas lines of the summer. People were asked to choose among three alternatives. One, a system of coupon rationing where all automobile drivers would be permitted to buy a particular number of gallons of gasoline every week, using ration coupons. That was the first choice—45 percent. The second choice—22 percent—was the following: allowing gasoline prices to increase so that vehicle usage would be discouraged and gasoline consumption would go down. This result again demonstrates that rationing is accepted in preference to price.

"The third and least favored alternative was the following: a system of allocation where each part of the country would be permitted only so much gasoline, and rationing would essentially take place as it did during the 1973-74 oil embargo—people would have to wait in line and stations would close when they ran out of gasoline. That experience was preferred by exactly 16 percent of the public. It did not want to see the experience repeated and, of course, within a few months, it was.

"This little piece of evidence suggests to me that the experience of rationing may be necessary in order to remove the impediments towards acceptance of a gas tax or higher prices.

"I'm not sure that the politics of this are very easy to explain. In the case of an emergency there might be justification for implementing rationing and the lesson would be learned in that case. Alternatively, if there were gas lines or serious shortages this summer, it might be sensible and in the long-term national interest for President Carter to implement a gas rationing plan for people to actually have the experience. In that case I think it would pave the way for President Reagan to implement the gas tax when he took office the following January."

Robert Allen of Lincoln, Mass., commented, "It seems to me that the Congress, if it is earning its pay, will in fact start to play the role of teacher if the emergency is as grave as people here have said it is."

"I don't see any way out of making radical changes to cure what I call the chronic emergency," replied Mr. Cooper. "But then I don't know that I think we ought to be in a hurry to put on a $2 gas tax to attack that chronic emergency. I think we need a gasoline rationing plan for the acute emergency and we need desperately to fill our strategic reserves and think about what kind of authority you want the President to have in those cases."

"We have heard here over and over again that time is considerably short," continued Mr. Allen. "Are these people wrong? Are we in the midst of a very urgent time?"

"Of course," Cooper said.

"How can we have a sense of leisure?" said Allen.

"It is a question of whether the solution you propose is more trouble than the problem itself," replied Cooper.

"I wanted to take a couple of minutes to sum up something as a foreigner, but a foreigner who is totally dependent on the good and welfare of this country," said David Melnik, Energy Adviser to the Province of Ontario. "Our concern in Canada is that you buy 25 percent of our gross national product, you have invested over $50 billion in Canada, and you cough and we get pneumonia. So it's a very, very serious problem for us to see what is happening in this country now.

"And what is happening, as we see it, is that you have lost your independence as long as you really are stuck with the crises over your oil supply. You're struggling to try to come to some formulation of policies that are going to make you independent. It's our hope that you'll do that, but in the meantime I perceive that what you're really doing is saying, 'We are going to have to have some changes in our way of life. Now, how are we going to do that, and can we do that?' The guy that wants to start a family and own his house, doesn't really care about the United States as world leader. I care very much about the United States as world leader because we are totally dependent on you to come to some resolution of these problems."

Ted Marmor presented a summary of the Symposium's discussion:

"I was struck by some elements of agreement," he said. "By the agreement about this distinction between the short and long term problem and the willingness of a good number of people representing Congress to see the foreign policy independence questions in a way that might be action-forcing. By contrast, I was struck by the absence of agreement that an external crisis might well be the occasion for pushing longer term solutions. I was struck also, I think, by the attention, the kind of serious review and the willingness to listen to the problems of implementation of a number of these proposals. I was struck by the extent to which people are willing to hear and certainly to express some notion about the interchangeability of some of these seemingly quite different proposals, the extent to which changing one or another feature can make them look somewhat more similar. Finally, I guess I was very much struck by the extent to which foreign policy security considerations or a change in the world could make this conversation speed up.

"Now, as to the disagreements. There was extraordinary disagreement about how reactive the institutions of our government are now. There was no agreement at all around the table as to whether the important thing to do is to tell the public, to try to educate it, or to respond to it.

"There certainly were intense disagreements about how we get from here to any longer term reduction of the demand— particularly since the short-run interruptions are unpredictable as to when they will take place. So, there is a lot of disagreement on that getting from here to there. It seems to me there has also been a lot of disagreement on how to interpret congressional behavior. That hasn't been explicitly dealt with. But we have heard a good deal of concern about the peculiarity of apparent agreement on the seriousness of the problem, but a seeming inability to respond.

"We ought not to be fooled by the use of the words 'energy crisis.' Beneath those words lie different conceptions of different parts of the population whose values count. The clash of values shows dramatically in people's view of who is going to gain and who is going to lose from a very complex chain of activities," said Marmor.

"The United States could well be living on borrowed time in terms of its energy supply," said Daniel Yergin in conclusion. "It would be reassuring if we could cast a ballot for President and go back to 33 cents a gallon gasoline, and benefit from price wars at filling stations. That is one choice, one option, that we do not have. That is over.

"The problem of dependence is likely to grow worse, not better, in the 1980s because of what now looks to be the rather steep decline in domestic oil production. Even if we improve our efficiencies, we could still end up importing more oil in 1985 than today. The hopes of a few years ago about increasing, or at least stabilizing, domestic production are unlikely to be realized. In other words, the real US energy policy could continue to be 'import oil.'

"What would be the costs? We have already seen some. America's *weekly* bill for imported oil increased from $800 million a week at the end of 1978 to $1.8 billion by March 22, 1980. These are dollars not being invested in the United States, but rather taxed away by OPEC. Current and growing levels of US imports increase the probability of similar price jumps in the future. Growing US imports will have very negative impact on American relations with Western Europe and Japan, and can directly and indirectly corrode fundamental security relationships. Moreover, such dependence sharply circumscribes US foreign policy. Interruption of oil supplies in such a state of over-dependence would have very severe direct implications for America's security. This country could find itself in a situation in which it has lost all flexibility to deal with uncertainties and contingencies in the world. America's overall strategic posture in the world is shaped at least as much by its oil-import levels as by the obvious military balance.

"In sum, there is a driving need to do something serious about American oil imports—and that need, in turn, focuses attention on gasoline. There are drawbacks to the various alternatives to current levels of gasoline consumption. There are problems of lead time, of implementation, of administration, of acceptability. Yet, depending on the mix of methods, the difficulties seem manageable, to varying degrees. A careful scrutiny of the two major tools—rationing and tax—leads to two conclusions: 1) rationing with marketable coupons is fundamentally quite similar to a tax with rebates. 2) A tax is sure to be less of a hassle for just about everybody.

"The worst thing is to do nothing. If that is the result, then one cannot help but imagine how historians in the future will write about this period—with irony, or with sheer disbelief that a society was not able to take steps so manifestly in its own interest.

"The era of cheap and easy oil—of cheap and easy gasoline—really and truly is over. It has been replaced by an era of expensive and insecure oil. This era grows progressively more dangerous for the United States. It does behoove the United States to take those steps that would enhance the safety and well-being of its people."

PART III

FORTY MILES A GALLON BY 1995 AT THE VERY LEAST: Why the US Needs a New Automotive Fuel Economy Goal
by Frank von Hippel

Background

Until recently, virtually all of our nation's energy planning has been built on the expectation that petroleum prices and the availability of petroleum will change slowly. Thus, the most recent (1978) *Annual Report to Congress* by the Department of Energy projected that gasoline prices would rise at a rate of only a few percent per year with a doubling occurring at the earliest by the year 1995. Such a projection must have seemed reasonably conservative in 1978 when gasoline prices had been declining for four straight years at an average rate of 2 percent a year (in constant dollars) since their "anomalous" 25 percent increase during the winter 1973-1974 Arab oil embargo. (See Figure 1.)

Figure 1

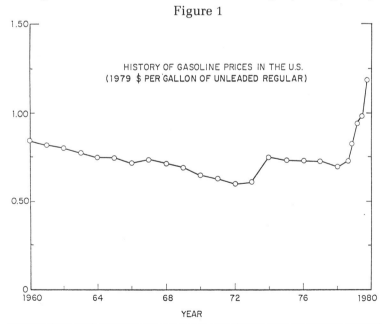

HISTORY OF GASOLINE PRICES IN THE U.S.
(1979 $ PER GALLON OF UNLEADED REGULAR)

YEAR

Frank von Hippel is Senior Research Scientist at the Center for Energy and Environmental Studies. He recieved his Ph.D. in theoretical physics from Oxford University in 1962. He is co-author with J. Primack of *Advice and Dissent.*

"*Attention all department heads: From now on, we're just going to make small, reliable cars.*"

During the last year, however, we have become aware of the many other ways in which petroleum exports from the Middle East could be disrupted, requiring our allies and ourselves to cut back consumption by millions of barrels per day. And we have had the experience of seeing even a relatively minor reduction in world supplies precipitate in our own country half a mile long gasoline lines and gasoline prices which are now expected to be at twice their 1978 levels in constant dollars by 1981.

The US consumes 30 percent of the total world production of petroleum. Obviously, to the extent that we can cut our thirst for this liquid, the less disruptive any sudden supply cutoff will be and the less serious the international crisis which will result.

These perceptions are not new. The Arab oil embargo six years ago also focused national attention on the vulnerability which had come with our increasing dependence on imported petroleum. As a result, Congress in 1975 targeted the single largest cause of our enormous consumption of petroleum: America's 100 million gas-guzzling automobiles. A law was passed which mandated a doubling of the average fuel economy of new US automobiles by 1985—to 27.5 miles per gallon. Intermediate goals were set by Congress for the years 1978-1980 and by the Secretary of Transportation for the years 1981-1984.

Prior to the gasoline price rises of 1979, the US automobile manufacturers tried to slow the Department of Transportation's implementation of the fuel economy law.[1] They were reluctant to spend more than the absolute minimum required for retooling—perhaps because they were convinced that they were being forced to make smaller and less powerful passenger cars than the American public really wanted. And Congress forgot the urgency that it had felt in 1975 about the need for fuel economy improvements. Some key Congressional committees even began to listen sympathetically to complaints from the auto manufacturers that the EPA and DOT were being too aggressive in implementing the fuel economy law.[2]

Early in 1979, however, as a result of the gasoline price increases and uncertainties about future gasoline supplies, new car buyers began demanding an average fuel economy which was both higher than Congress had mandated and higher than Detroit could supply. A year later, despite the lay-offs of over 200,000 auto workers, despite heavy promotion of their big cars and trucks, and despite steep price increases on their fast-selling fuel-efficient vehicles,[3] the domestic auto manufacturers had still not succeeded in getting their inventories back in balance.

In each size class the models in shortest supply were the
models with the best EPA "estimated" (city) fuel economy. The
preference for good fuel economy was much less marked in the
case of mid-sized and large cars, but large cars as a class were
becoming less popular—falling from 22 percent of the new car
market in 1978 to 18 percent in 1979, while the combined share
held by subcompacts and minicompacts increased from 30 to 40
percent.[4]

The same kind of size class shift was being felt in the light
truck sales. Total sales of light trucks declined by one million
between 1978 and 1979, but sales of smaller light trucks—many
of them imports—actually increased by 100,000.[5]

While Detroit's inability to sell its large vehicles dropped 1979
sales of domestic cars below 1978 levels by one million, sales of
imported cars rose by more than 300,000[6]—with the result that
the import share of the US new car market rose to record levels.
(See Figure 2.)

It is generally agreed that, without the pressure of the federal
fuel economy standards, Detroit would have been caught even
more unprepared for the sudden market demand for energy
efficient vehicles.

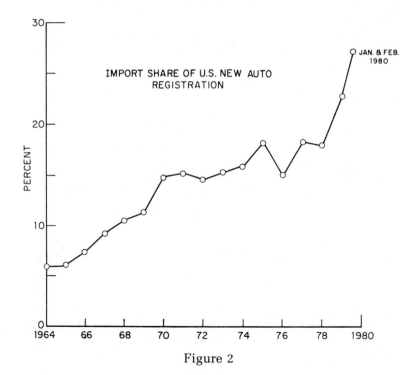

Figure 2

It is now only five years till 1985—not a long time in comparison to Detroit's planning horizon—and it would appear timely for the Congress to address the question of post-1985 automotive fuel economy standards. In the absence of new initiatives, the federal minimum standard would remain at 27.5 mpg as measured by the EPA test. Data for 1974-1978 model automobiles indicate that this may correspond to only approximately 20 mpg on the road (see also Figure 3).[7]

The Jackson-Magnuson Proposal

Recently, 12 Senators led by Senators Jackson and Magnuson took the first initiatives to propose post-1985 automotive fuel economy standards. The Senators propose that by 1995 the minimum average automotive fuel economy of new cars should rise to 40 miles per gallon on the road.

Such a fuel economy target is obviously achievable. Since 1977 VW has been selling the diesel Rabbit, which has a fuel economy of about 42 mpg on the road, almost three times the current US average.[8] Although the Rabbit's exterior dimensions are smaller than what we became accustomed to in the era of large American cars, the hatchback version is less than 20 percent smaller than the average US car when measured in terms of interior space.[9]

National and international security and economic interests require that we effect as rapid a reduction of our petroleum

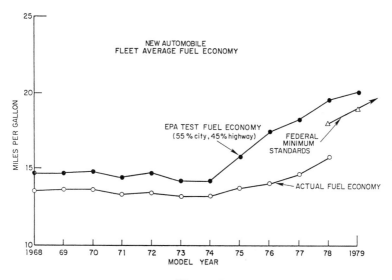

Figure 3

consumption as possible. It may well turn out, therefore, as the proposed standards are considered further and the major technology opportunities for going well beyond the VW Rabbit technology become clearer, that the Senators have chosen a 1995 target that is too low.[10] VW has already tested a 4-passenger car with an advanced small diesel engine and obtained an EPA composite fuel economy in excess of 70 mpg (see below). The company is also developing, in a four-year program funded in part by the West German government, a lightweight low-drag automobile larger than the Rabbit which is expected to get a fuel economy "in excess of 65 mpg" and to satisfy "all other requirements with respect to pollution and to vehicle safety."[11]

The Problem of Gas Guzzling Light Trucks

Thus far no new legislation has been proposed which addresses the question of post-1985 fuel economy standards for light trucks (pickups, vans etc.). During the past few years, for every ten new automobiles sold, three new light trucks have also been sold. (See Figure 4.) These vehicles loom even larger in the nation's gasoline consumption picture than their numbers indicate because they use more fuel per mile on average than cars. Because light trucks have such diverse uses, Congress did not establish any numerical fuel economy standards for them but

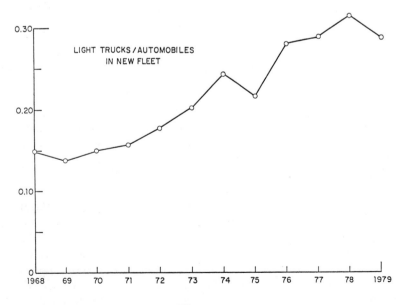

Figure 4

instead gave the authority to do so to the Secretary of Transportation. The DOT has, however, been indecisive in implementing this authority; to date it has delayed its decisions on each model year until it was so late that it could do little to influence the plans of the manufacturers.[12] Since light trucks are used principally for the same purposes as passenger cars,[13] the result is a major loophole in the fuel economy standards that should be more effectively addressed by both the DOT and Congress.

Below I discuss in more detail why post-1985 automotive and light truck fuel economy standards are both necessary and practical. I also discuss some of the issues which they raise.

The Potential Savings

If our current fleet of 100 million automobiles were getting an average of 40 mpg instead of about 15 mpg on the road, US petroleum imports would be reduced by almost 3 million barrels a day. If the fuel economy of our current fleet of 30 million light trucks were improved by a corresponding factor to 30 mpg from about 12 mpg on the road, we would be able to forgo the import of another one million barrels a day (see Figure 5).[14] The 4 million barrels a day total reduction would correspond to about one half of our current level of imports—or alternatively, the total petroleum consumption of Latin America,—or alternatively, three times the total petroleum consumption of China. If, as is usually assumed, population growth and increasing affluence drive up the level of light vehicle miles traveled in the future, the savings would increase correspondingly.

The Market for Fuel Economy

Some analysts oppose higher post-1985 fuel economy standards. They object, on principle, to a regulatory approach to the gas guzzler problem. "Let the market do it," they say, pointing to the fact that the recent increase in the price of gasoline has created a market demand for increased fuel economy.

What about the market? In 1976 it cost an estimated 20 cents per mile (in 1979 dollars) to operate a "standard" size automobile. At an average on-road fuel economy of 13.5 mpg, only about 5 cents per mile went to the purchase of gasoline costing about 70 cents per gallon (1979 dollars).[15] Assuming gasoline climbs in the next year or so to twice the 1976 price in constant dollars, the cost of operating this same car (other things being equal) would climb to 25 cents per mile (1979 dollars). This would create a market incentive for the average car owner to buy a more fuel efficient car next time—but how much more fuel-efficient?

Figure 5

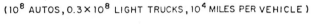

RATE OF PETROLEUM CONSUMPTION BY TWO LIGHT
VEHICLE FLEETS

(10^8 AUTOS, 0.3×10^8 LIGHT TRUCKS, 10^4 MILES PER VEHICLE)

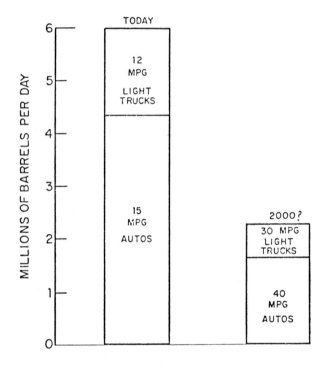

If he or she were able to go out and buy a new car which was identical to the old car except that it got twice the on-road fuel economy (27 mpg), then the gasoline costs would be reduced back down to 5 cents per mile and presumably the car owner would be as happy as before. But a doubling of fuel economy cannot ordinarily be obtained without cost. The new car would probably be either more expensive (in constant dollars) than the old one, or smaller. As a consequence, the new car buyer would probably end up "splitting the difference" and buy a new car with less than twice the fuel economy of the old one. (In the economist's jargon this would correspond to the "elasticity" of the demand for new car fuel economy as a function of gasoline price being less than unity.) And, indeed, when in the mid-1970s European gasoline prices were approximately at the current US level,[16] the average fuel economy of European automobiles was only about 21 miles per gallon as measured on the road.[17] This would correspond to an average EPA composite fuel economy probably slightly higher than the 1985 US standards of 27.5 mpg.

From this perspective there appears to be no rational predictable basis for the automobile manufacturers to expect new car buyers to demand an average on-road fuel economy greater than 40 mpg by the year 1995. And, if they do not expect it, they will not tool up to produce such vehicles. Consequently, under these circumstances, even if it turns out that new car buyers want 40+ mpg cars in 1995, they will be unable to purchase them in large numbers (from domestic manufacturers at least).

A recent *Automotive News* story gives one indication of what Detroit thinks that the future market will demand. It reports that the Pontiac Division of General Motors has just "pumped 8 million into the. . . .development budget" of a new two seater "commuter car." According to the specifications given in the story, this commuter will be heavier than, and have an engine with almost twice the power of, the VW Rabbit diesel. The story continues: "In addition, Pontiac engineers are working on a sportier, high-performance version of the commuter" which would be equipped with an even more powerful engine.[18]

The following anecdote may also serve to indicate Detroit's disinterest, based on its present view of the market, in even investigating important efficiency improvements. Recently, I attended a meeting at which engineering representatives from both Volkswagen and a Detroit auto manufacturer were present. During lunch I discussed with the man from Detroit the proposed 40 miles per gallon average standard for 1995 automobiles. He responded flatly that it was not feasible.

After the lunch the group reconvened, and one of the engineers from VW mentioned that his company had installed in a four passenger car a small three cylinder supercharged diesel engine which shuts off under coasting or idle conditions and had measured an EPA composite fuel economy of "70 to 80 miles per gallon." Most of us were unaware that VW had actually put together a vehicle with such a high fuel economy.[19] This news therefore caused some excitement. The engineer from VW hastened to add that the vehicle was not ready for mass production—for one thing, he said, "the idle is unacceptably rough." He did agree, however, that VW could certainly market a vehicle with such a fuel economy by the 1990s. At this point, the man from Detroit broke in and said: "Sure, so could we, but who would want to buy such a car?"

We simply do not know what percentage of Americans would be interested in a relatively low performance 70-80 mpg subcompact today. However, each gasoline shortage and/or price hike in the future is likely to increase that percentage—especially among the approximately 75 percent of American new car buyers who belong to households which own two or more cars.[20] More and more of us are likely to begin to believe that our choice may be one of having such a small car or not being able to get where we want to go. But, based on past experience, it is quite possible that, when the demand materializes on a large scale, Detroit will once again be caught by surprise and will only then start to tool up. I would once more like to quote the engineer from Detroit: "If by any chance you want us to be producing cars like that by 1995, you had better let us know soon!"

If the nation's security demands that the average fuel economy of US automobiles be raised over 40 miles per gallon, it will be necessary for the federal government to institute policies which will encourage automobile buyers to want more fuel efficient vehicles and which will also ensure that the automobile manufacturers will start tooling up to produce these vehicles without undue delay.

Market Forcing

One obvious way to give new car buyers a stronger incentive to take into account the national interest in reducing gasoline consumption would be to introduce in the US a stiff gasoline tax such as the Europeans have had for years. New car buyers could largely escape the effect of this tax by moving to more fuel efficient vehicles. The problem is of course how to soften the blow to those who would have to wait until these fuel efficient vehicles became available in the used car market. This complex subject has been explored elsewhere.[21]

How far a gasoline tax will push new car buyers toward fuel economy in the absence of other policies is uncertain, however. And uncertainty would make Detroit reluctant to make investments in dramatic fuel economy gains. Instead, Detroit would tend to "play it safe" and make smaller incremental investments in a series of relatively modest fuel economy improvements—an approach which would be much slower and ultimately much more expensive than a 10-15 year program systematically directed toward the achievement of a specific fuel economy target.

The role of fuel economy standards would therefore be to supplement a gasoline tax by making a clear national commitment to a specific minimum target. The auto manufacturer who produced fuel efficient vehicles would then be protected from competitors who might otherwise try to compete as in the past by promoting a line of heavy cars which are "loaded with power."

Technology Forcing

When new car buyers decided in the middle of model year 1979 (March) that they wanted to reduce their gasoline costs, one of their principal tactics was to buy a smaller car. Despite the technological opportunities which have been demonstrated in the VW Rabbit diesel, the differences between the fuel economies of the small and large cars made by US auto companies are surprisingly small. As a result, the chaos in the new car market caused by the shift to small cars had a surprisingly small payoff in increased energy efficiency: only one mile per gallon average composite EPA fuel economy improvement between the first and second halves of the model year 1979.[22]

Fortunately, however, at the same time that Detroit was under pressure from the market to produce more small cars, it was also under pressure from the federal fuel economy standards to improve the energy efficiency of all its cars in ways that would be undetectable to most new car buyers. The payoff from this "technology forcing" became visible in September 1979 when the model year 1980 cars came out. In order to meet the stiffer model year 1980 minimum Corporate Average Fuel Economy (CAFE) standards, the auto manufacturers had cut the weight and improved the aerodynamics of their cars. They had also installed smaller engines, better transmissions, better carburetors and lower rolling resistance tires.[23] As a result, the EPA fuel economy of each 1980 car was an average 2 miles per gallon higher than that of the 1979 car which it replaced. The fuel economy effects of these technological improvements and the market shift were additive and the average composite EPA fuel economy of the new car fleet sold during the first four months of model year 1980 was almost three miles per gallon higher than that of the model year 1979 fleet.[24]

This experience makes clear once again that, even if there is a strong market demand for fuel economy, if the manufacturers drag their heels in making design improvements, new car buyers will get a lot less than they are asking for. Tough fuel economy standards help force the pace of technological improvement.

Making the Market Predictable for Detroit

In a situation of uncertainty concerning the future demand for fuel economy, it might be expected that an industry which has traditionally minimized its capital investments in new technology (as opposed to style changes) will not invest in the tooling required to make fuel-efficient automobiles. For the nation, however, such a strategy of following the market is unacceptable. It takes approximately ten years to replace our fleet of automobiles. If we add a five year delay for Detroit to catch up with the new car buyers, the fuel economy of the automobile fleet on the road will always be fifteen years behind what new car buyers are demanding. Events may just move too rapidly for us to have the luxury of such a long adjustment period without major disruptions in our economy and potentially serious international confrontations resulting from petroleum shortages.

We must therefore make sure that Detroit does not waste any more time waiting to see that a market really will exist for cars which get better than 40 miles per gallon. This can only be done by setting a national fuel economy target such as that proposed by Senator Jackson and his colleagues. If this target is backed by a stiff gasoline tax, then the market for fuel economy will have been made predictable for Detroit, and the auto manufacturers will be able to focus on building cars which are as energy efficient as the national security requires. (A potential additional benefit to US auto workers and auto manufacturers of such a strategy is that, if our national fuel economy standards push US automobile technology beyond that of Europe and Japan, we might see a demand for US cars develop in those countries.)

Why Not Synthetic Fuels Instead?

It is often suggested that a more economical alternative to retooling the US automobile industry to produce "gas sipping" cars would be to invest the money in building plants which would produce gasoline from coal and alcohol from corn as a substitute for imported oil.

As far as alcohol is concerned, any likely level of supply would not propel America's current fleet of gas guzzlers very far. Even if all the corn grown in the US were fermented into ethanol, it would still supply less than one-fifth of the energy consumed in US automobiles today.[25] If US cars become much more fuel-efficient, however, the potential significance of fuels derived from biomass will become correspondingly larger.

Synthetic fuels could eventually be produced from coal, oil shale, etc., in sufficient quantities to fuel our gas guzzlers but probably only at a cost much greater than that which would be required to shift Detroit over to the production of energy efficient light cars and trucks. In fact, the proposed *federal contribution* of up to $88 billion to help start up a US synthetic fuels industry which would by 1992 produce "the equivalent of at least 2 million barrels of oil per day of synthetic fuels" would by itself be more than enough to pay the *entire cost* of retooling the US automobile industry to produce fuel-efficient automobiles and light trucks.

The DOT's Transportation Systems Center has estimated that the total cost for retooling the US automotive industry "for a continued post-1985 increase in motor vehicle fuel economy to a mid-1990s level of 40-50 miles per gallon for passenger cars and 25-35 miles per gallon for light trucks with a resulting saving of 2-3 million barrels per day in the year 2000," would require capital investments of 67 billion (1979) dollars.[26]

Any requirement for government aid over this period would presumably be much less, since, in the absence of rising federal fuel economy standards, the industry could be expected to invest on the order of $50 billion over the same ten-year period (1985-1995) in routine repair and replacement of its production capacity.[27] (This, of course, is the principal rationale for giving Detroit a ten to fifteen year lead time to phase in the production capacity for fuel-efficient light vehicles. Over this period Detroit would ordinarily go through major retooling programs to produce two new "generations" of vehicles[28] and much of the plant and equipment not affected by these design changes would become obsolete and have to be replaced. As a result, the incremental costs of introducing fuel economy improvements in the course of all this turnover of capital equipment would be much reduced.)

Without outside assistance, however, Detroit might have difficulty in raising the capital it will need to retool. It is important therefore to assess and to begin public discussions as to whether such assistance will be required.

Even if it were no less expensive than the development of synthetic fuels, a strategy based on light vehicle fuel economy improvements would still be preferable, both because of the pollution associated with fossil fuel production and consumption and because of considerations of international equity.

Locally, pollution problems would be reduced because in most cases they are directly proportional to the amounts of fossil fuels being produced (at refineries, synfuel plants, coal mines, etc.) or being burned. Globally, we know that the current level of global fossil fuel use is leading to a build-up of carbon dioxide in the atmosphere toward a level that climatologists fear will result in major changes in the global climate during the next century. If we can cut our consumption of fossil fuels by increasing the efficiency of their use, therefore, we will be buying extra time for the world to make the necessary transition to other energy sources.

Considerations of international equity arise because it does not appear likely that with current technology the global environment could tolerate a level of energy use by the other peoples of the world at the current US per capita rate. To the extent, therefore, that we reduce our energy use by efficiency improvements, our society will be coming closer to being a model which the rest of the world can realistically emulate without precipitating an environmental catastrophe.

What Could Go Wrong?

There are of course some potential hazards associated with stiff national fuel economy standards. These include: possible rejection by the market, the safety issues associated with small cars, and the air pollution problems associated with diesels.

Market Rejection: Prior to the 1979 market shift, Detroit was arguing that the government was forcing it to make smaller automobiles than the public wanted, that many new car buyers might therefore decide to hold on to their old cars for a year or two longer, and that, as a result, more than one hundred thousand auto workers might lose their jobs.[29] Of course, just the opposite happened with worse results: the US market rejected Detroit's big cars because they were not fuel-efficient enough and over 200,000 auto workers lost their jobs. What if, however, Detroit's nightmare about getting ahead of the market came true?

Not surprisingly, the Congress in 1975 built more than ample safeguards into the fuel economy law to protect the automobile companies from serious damage if the standards should turn out for any reason to be too ambitious. The Jackson-Magnuson proposal would maintain and even increase these protections. The Secretary of Transportation would be authorized to lower the 1995 fuel economy standard to 35 mpg and could lower it still further subject only to a one-House congressional veto. Furthermore, the penalty for a company which did not achieve the fuel economy standards would continue to be a civil penalty of $50 per car per mpg of shortfall—hardly a draconian amount[30]—and even that penalty could be reduced on the recommendation of the Federal Trade Commission for a manufacturer in serious financial trouble.

Finally, in the absence of a discovery that the Great Lakes are actually filled with oil, it is unlikely that there will be any sudden shift of consumer demand toward *less* efficient cars. Since the increase of the fuel economy standards will be relatively gradual—about 1-2 mpg per year if we have a target of 40 mpg by the year 1995—any situation in which the fuel economy standards get ahead of the market will develop relatively slowly, giving ample time for corrective action before a serious gap can open up.

Any concerns about market rejection due to overshooting the consumer demand for fuel efficiency are likely to remain as groundless in the future as they have been in the past. If the world's future petroleum situation continues to look as serious as it does now, it is all too likely that the nation's problem will continue to be getting Detroit to move ahead nearly quickly enough.

Safety: Concern is often expressed that the trend towards smaller cars will result in a higher automobile accident fatality rate. Indeed, this concern is shared widely enough so that it may be slowing the market shift. Paradoxically, although most Americans refuse to use their automobile seat belts, many of them justify buying larger, heavier cars than they need because they believe that larger cars are safer.

It is certainly true that today, in collisions between typical large and small cars, the occupants of the small cars are much more likely to be killed.[31] For this reason the National Highway Traffic Safety Administration (NHTSA) has, over the past few years, consistently pushed for safety related design improvements—especially in small cars. Some recent progress in this area is indicated by the fact that, of the four model year 1980 US cars which NHTSA found provided "adequate" protection for seatbelted passengers in 35 mph front and rear crashes into fixed barriers (the legal requirement is such protection at 30 mph), two were subcompacts (the Plymouth Horizon and the Ford Mustang) and another was one of GM's radically downsized X-body cars.

Obviously any national commitment to higher fuel economy standards should be accompanied by a renewed national commitment to increased automotive safety.

Diesel Pollution: The issue of diesel pollution is currently also quite controversial. Diesel engines are today 20-30 percent more fuel-efficient than spark ignition engines,[32] but they also emit about one hundred times the weight of small particles, and the particles carry carcinogens of as yet unknown potency.[33]

Fortunately, once again, it appears that it is possible to mitigate this problem. Exhaust gas treatment devices are being tested by the Environmental Protection Agency which are expected to make possible a reduction of diesel particulate emissions down to at least one third of their current level. If, as we learn more about this pollution problem it appears that the level of control attainable with these systems and other technological improvements is still not adequate, then it is likely that small versions of engines like the "PROCO" stratified charge spark ignition engine currently being fleet tested by Ford will offer a clean energy efficient alternative to the diesel.

Conclusion

It appears that the time has come to retire American gas guzzlers in favor of smaller, more efficient vehicles which will provide us with the transportation we need without consuming more fuel than is consistent with a stable international political situation. Higher fuel prices are pushing us in this direction, but not predictably enough for either the national security or Detroit's long term product planning. We need federal fuel economy standards, and the automobile industry may need federal help in raising the capital that will be required to retool to meet these standards.

Acknowledgement

I wish to thank Dr. Margaret Fels of Princeton University's Center for Energy and Environmental Studies, who first introduced me to the fuel economy issue and who has been most generous in sharing with me her library and contacts.

NOTES

1. See, e.g., U.S. DOT, *Report on Requests by General Motors and Ford to Reduce Fuel Economy Standards for MY 1981-85 Passenger Automobiles* (DOT HS-804 731), June 1979.

2. See, e.g., *Motor Vehicle Fuel Efficiency*, Hearings before the Subcommittee on Energy and Power of the House Committee on Interstate and Foreign Affairs, March 13 and 14, 1979.

3. The latest price hike by GM averaged 2.2 percent and ranged from 4 percent on the X-body cars (Buick Skylark, Oldsmobile Omega, Chevrolet Citation, and Pontiac Phoenix), and 3.7 percent for the Chevette—all cars at or near the top of the fuel economy range in their size classes—to no increase for the Chevrolet Camero which is near the bottom of the subcompact fuel economy range. *Automotive News* noted that:

> "The X-cars have had a rather fantastic history of price increases ever since they were introduced on April 19, 1979.
>
> They are GM's best selling models and the corporation has boosted them accordingly. In less than a year, the new front-wheel-drive compacts have jumped an average of $954 or 19.98 percent over their introductory stickers."

(John K. Teaken Jr., "GM Increases Prices by an Average of $186; 2.2 Pct. Hike Had Been Expected," *Automotive News*, April 7, 1980, p. 3.)

4. Unweighted averages over calendar year, 1978 and 1979 market shares [David L. Green *et. al.* "Monthly MPG and Market Share (3MS) Data System," Oak Ridge National Laboratory, Jan. 22, 1980.]

5. "Light Truck Registrations off 12.5 pct.: Domestic Light Trucks Suffer Most in '79," *Automotive News*, February 25, 1980, p. 8. (Small light trucks are those under 6000 pounds gross vehicle weight.)

6. Jenny L. King, "Final New-Car Tallies for '79: Domestic Slide Began in March," *Automotive News*, January 14, 1980, p. 2.

7. In a recent DOE survey of the in-use fuel economy of model years 1974-78 automobiles the following "best fit" relationship was obtained between the in-use fuel economy (Y) to EPA composite fuel economy (X): $Y^{-1} = 0.765 \times X^{-1} + 0.024$. For $X = 27.5$ mpg this relationship gives us $Y = 19.3$ mpg. [Barry D. McNutt *et. al.* (DOE), "Comparison of EPA and In-use Fuel Economy of 1974-1978 Automobiles," Society of Automotive Engineers Paper #790932 (1979)]. The 1974-1979 new car fleets had the following average estimated EPA composite fuel economies: 1974—14.2; 1975—15.8; 1976—17.5; 1977—18.3; 1978—19.6; and 1979—20.1. The estimated in-use fuel economy of the 1974-1979 fleets at 4000 miles were: 1974—13.2; 1975—13.8; 1976—14.1; 1977—14.7; and 1978—15.8. For the model year 1979 fleets, information on in-use fuel economy is only available from GM and Ford. These preliminary data indicate that the in-use fuel economy of the model year 1979 fleet will be in the range 15.7-17.2 mpg. [Ref. EPA, Draft Report to Congress, *Passenger Car Fuel Economy: EPA and Road* (January 1980).]

8. The measured EPA composite fuel economy of the VW Rabbit diesel equipped with a five speed manual transmission is 47 mpg. (EPA, *Test Car List* used to compile the *1980 Gas Mileage Guide*.) The best fit relationship between EPA (X) and on-road (Y) fuel economy obtained for diesel powered vehicles by McNutt *et. al.* (Note 7) is $Y^{-1} = 1.17 X^{-1} - 0.001$. At $X = 47$ mpg this relationship gives $Y = 42$ mpg.

9. J.D. Murrell (EPA), "Light Duty Automotive Fuel Economy. . .Trends Through 1979," SAE Paper #790225 (1979).

10. Jake Kelderman, "U.S. Study Urges 85 MPG Average for 1995 Models," *Automotive News*, April 7, 1980, p. 1.

11. VW's program to develop a "Research Vehicle 2000 with a size between the compact and subcompact class [an] inertia weight [curb weight plus 300 pounds] of 1730 lbs. . . . an airdrag area smaller than 0.55 m², [and a] 1.2 liter supercharged Diesel using a control system which stops the engine at idling and deceleration modes, [which] is expected to attain a combined cycle fuel economy of more than 65 mpg . . . together with . . . all the other requirements with respect to pollutant emissions and to vehicle safety" is described in U. Seiffert *et. al.* (VW) "Improvements in Automotive Fuel Economy," (paper presented at the First International Fuel Economy Research Conference, Washington, D.C., October 31-November 1, 1979).

12. Thus, for example, the fuel economy standards for model year 1982 light trucks which will be marketed beginning in September 1981 were only finalized in March 1980. Standards for model years 1983-1985 are expected soon, however. (Helen Kahn, "Fuel Standard for Light Trucks Placed at 18 MPG for 1982," *Automotive News*, March 31, 1980, p. 1.)

13. One adjustable parameter in the EPA fuel economy test is the average load which the vehicle is expected to carry. In the case of automobiles, this average load is assumed to be the driver plus one passenger, each of average weight, for a total average load of 300 pounds. In preparing the regulations for the light truck tests for model year 1978, the EPA proposed that, because they are bought for their load carrying or hauling capabilities, it should be assumed for purposes of the tests that light trucks carry on average a total load of 500 pounds. When this proposal was attacked by the manufacturers, however, EPA could find no data to support the position that on average light trucks carry more load than passenger cars and therefore ended up assuming for fuel economy testing purposes that they carry the same average load. [Action Memorandum, EPA, Ann Arbor, "Regulations for 1978 and Later Model Year Light Trucks" (1976).]

14. In 1979, there were an estimated 104 million cars and 29 million light trucks (pickups, vans etc. of less than 10,000 pounds Gross Vehicle Weight) registered in the U.S. [Barry McNutt *et. al.* (US DOE), "On-Road Fuel Economy Trends and Impacts," Feb. 17, 1979 as updated April 19, 1979.] In 1977, US automobiles traveled an average of about 9,800 miles and "single unit" trucks (mostly light trucks) traveled an average of 9,400 miles. The average fuel economy of the automobiles was estimated at 13.9 miles per gallon and of the single unit trucks 10.1 miles per gallon. [US DOT, *Highway Statistics*, 1977 (FHWA-HP-HS-77), p. 100.] I have increased these fuel economy numbers in the text to reflect improvements since 1977 and to compensate for the lowering effect of trucks (over 10,000 pounds Gross Vehicle Weight) on the average fuel economy of single unit trucks.

15. US DOT, *National Transportation Statistics*, 1979, p. 100. We have converted 1976 to 1979 dollars, using a GNP inflator of 1.125 taken from *Economic Indicators*.

16. In June 1975 some European prices of regular gasoline per gallon (converted at March 1, 1979 exchange rates) were: France—$1.50, Italy—$1.29, United Kingdom—$1.18, and West Germany—$1.70 (CIA, *International Statistical Review*, 12 March, 1980, p. 20.)

17. General Motors has estimated, from 1976 Belgian, German, and Swedish fuel consumption data, an overall in-use automobile fuel economy of 21 miles

per gallon. [Reed M. Brown (G.M.) *Overseas Automotive Fuel Economy Study* (Environmental Activities Publication No. A-3678, 1978).]

18. Jim Plegue, "Pontiac Grooms Mid-Engine, 2-Seat Commuter," *Automotive News,* January 28, 1980, p. 1.

19. A VW supercharged 1.2 liter three cylinder diesel engine which turns off during deceleration and idle is mentioned briefly in the January 28, 1980 *Automotive News* (p. 16) story by Jan P. Norbye, "VW Spends Big on Total Energy Research: All its Projects Have Definite Goals."

20. In 1976, 52 percent of all US households owned two or more cars. Among households purchasing new cars, 75.9 percent owned two or more cars (U.S. News and World Report Marketing Department, *Automotive Market: 1977 Report.*)

21. See, e.g., R.H. Williams, "A $2 Per Gallon Political Opportunity" in this volume.

22. Difference between the average composite EPA fuel economies of the new cars sold in the US during the periods September 1978-February 1979 and March-August 1979 (not adjusted for differences in monthly sales totals) [David L. Greene *et. al.,* "Monthly MPG and Market Share (3 MS) Data System," Oak Ridge National Laboratory, January 22, 1980].

23. Roger Rowand, "No Magic, No Miracles in Boosting Economy: Solid, Down-to-Earth Engineering Gives '80 Models Better MPG," *Automotive News,* October 22, 1979.

24. Difference in the average composite EPA fuel economies of the new cars sold in the US during the periods September 1978-August 1979 and September-December 1979 (not adjusted for differences in monthly sales totals) [David Greene *et. al.,* op. cit. in ref. 35].

25. One bushel of corn would yield approximately 2.6 gallons of ethanol [gross, not net yield (US DOE, *The Report of the Alcohol Fuels Policy Review,* DOE/PE-0012, p. 13, 1979)]. Production of corn in the US in 1978 totaled 7 billion bushels (US DOC, *Statistical Abstract of the United States,* 1979, p. 709). The consumption of gasoline by US automobiles in 1977 was 80 billion gallons [US DOT, Highway Statistics, 1977 (FHWA-HP-HS-77), p. 100]. The energy content of a gallon of ethanol is approximately two thirds of that in a gallon of gasoline.

26. Richard R. John (DOT), "Transition to the Post-1985 Motor Vehicle," (First International Automotive Fuel Economy Research Conference, Washington, D.C., October 31-November 1, 1979). Included is the estimated cost of expanding the production capacity of the industry by 16 percent between 1985 and 1995. The higher end of the quoted mid-1990s fuel economy range assumes a complete shift to diesel engines.

27. In 1979, General Motors estimated that its average annual rate of capital investment to "repair, replace capacity, etc.," in the absence of "government mandated" investments in fuel economy, pollution control and safety improvements would be $2.9 billion. (G.M., "Economic Issues and Alternatives Associated With the Fuel Economy Program," February 1, 1979, Exhibit I.) In 1979 GM, sold 56 percent of all domestically produced vehicles. At GM's rate of investment per car sold, the total US automobile industry would therefore have invested approximately $5 billion annually. Over the ten-year investment period (1985-1995) investment at this rate would accumulate to approximately $50 billion.

28. In a study funded by General Motors, it is stated that "The major vehicle redesign year . . . generally occurs in a cycle of six to eight years—at GM it is five to six years." (Boston, Harbridge House Inc., *Energy Conservation and the Passenger Car,* September 1979.)

29. See, e.g., "Statement of General Motors to the National Highway Traffic Administration on 1981-84 Passenger Automobile Average Fuel Economy Standards," reprinted in *Energy Conservation-Motor Vehicles' Fuel Efficiency,* Hearings before the Subcommittee on Energy and Power of the House Committee on Interstate and Foreign Commerce, U.S. Congress, April 25, 1977, pp. 247-248.

30. One perspective on the magnitude of the civil penalty can be obtained by considering it to be a "gas tax" on the extra gasoline which would be consumed as a result of the shortfall. For a shortfall of one mpg the extra gasoline consumption in a 100,000 mile automobile lifetime relative to a fuel economy level of 20, 30, or 40 mpg would be about 260, 115, or 65 gallons respectively. The $50 fine imposed by the fuel economy law would therefore correspond to a tax of 20, 45 or 75 cents per gallon. (It is interesting to note that the increasing fuel economy standards tend to offset the eroding effect of inflation on this "gas tax.")

31. Statistics collected by the National Highway Traffic Safety Administration indicate "that in crashes involving subcompacts and larger cars, 85 percent of the persons killed were riding in the subcompacts." ('79 Highway Toll Rises to 50,745: Small Cars Deadlier Than Big, Claybrook Reports," Automotive News, April 7, 1980, p. 22).

32. See the survey of comparative results in E.G. Barry et. al., "If Autos Go to Diesel Fuel," in Hydrocarbon Processing, May 1977, p. 111. Comparison of gasoline and diesel fuel economy are made on a volume basis in this review. Diesel fuel #2 contains approximately 15 percent more energy per gallon than gasoline, but the EPA has concluded that shifting the refinery mix toward diesel would save the energy equivalent of approximately 0.1 gallons of gasoline in refinery process energy per gallon of refinery output shifted from gasoline to diesel fuel. The EPA has therefore decided to treat gasoline and diesel fuel as representing the same amount of crude oil per gallon. [US EPA, Technical Support Report for Regulatory Action, Method for Calculation of Diesel Fuel to Gasoline Fuel Economy Equivalence Factor, (May 1976)].

33. See, e.g., South Coast Technology Inc., "Unregulated Diesel Emissions and Their Potential Health Effects," in US DOT, Automotive Fuel Economy Contractors Coordination Meeting, Dec. 11-13, 1978, Summary Report (DOT HS-803 706), p. 1-4-1.

GASOLINE CONSUMPTION IN AN ERA OF CONFRONTATION

by William U. Chandler and Holly L. Gwin

1. Rumors of War

We have entered a new era of confrontation unprepared. The United States imports between 8 and 8.5 million barrels of oil per day; a quarter of this comes through the Strait of Hormuz, that narrow and vulnerable waterway between Iran and Saudi Arabia—only 400 miles from Afghanistan—through which 40 percent of the oil produced in the "free world" passes. If the flow of 16 million barrels of oil per day through the Strait were halted, the effect on Western nations would be staggering. The United States would lose 13 percent of its total oil supply; West Germany, 31 percent; Great Britain, 39 percent; France, 83 percent and Japan, 71 percent each. (See Table 1.) The effect of sharing losses of this magnitude with its Western allies (as required under international agreement)—combined with the stress that would be placed on the world oil market and an inevitably tense political situation in the region—would create problems for the United States out of proportion to the amount of oil that it would lose directly.[1]

The regional instability is certainly clear. The United States has declared the Strait of Hormuz and the Persian Gulf to be vital to its interests. After the Afghanistan invasion, the possibility of a direct Soviet-American confrontation over Middle Eastern oil becomes more real. Yet the United States is ill-prepared to

Table 1

Oil Movements through the Strait of Hormuz (1979)

Country	Oil received via the Strait of Hormuz	Percent of Total Oil Supply
	(Million barrels per day)	
France	1.9	83
Japan	4.0	71
United Kingdom	0.7	39
United States	2.4	13
West Germany	0.9	31

Source: Note 1

William U. Chandler, director of the Energy Conservation Project at the Environmental Policy Institute, is co-author with John H. Gibbons of *Energy: The Conservation Revolution*. Holly L. Gwin is a Washington, D.C., attorney.

deal with an emergency shortage of oil or to reduce oil consumption in order to prevent such an emergency. This article evaluates the policy tools which could be applied to ameliorate or to avert an oil shortage crisis in the United States, and thereby help avoid a larger confrontation.

1.1 How Much Reduction Is Necessary?

About two million barrels of oil per day come to the United States through the Strait of Hormuz. Iran, in mid-1979, produced roughly 3.5 million barrels of oil per day, about two million barrels per day less than before the Islamic Revolution. More recently, Iranian exports have fallen again to as low as 1.7 million barrels per day. If the United States were to decrease its consumption by an amount equal to the Iranian shortfall—thereby adding a "new supply" equivalent to the production of Kuwait to the world market—it could gain flexibility in foreign policy, reducing pressure on the price of oil, and perhaps still the rumors of war. A reduction of oil consumption by two million barrels per day, amounting to about ten percent of United States petroleum demand, or five percent of total United States energy demand, would not eliminate the strategic importance of the Persian Gulf; but it could significantly reduce world tension.

1.2 Where Should This Reduction Occur?

The primary target for reducing oil consumption in the United States might be in the largest single use of gasoline, used primarily in automobiles and light trucks. (Table 2 offers a description of the use of private automobiles for commuting, family business, and recreation.) Demand for diesel fuel in the US averages between .9 and 1 million barrels a day. The average passenger car, of which there are about 100 million in operation in the United States, travels almost 10,000 miles per year, consuming about 700 gallons of gasoline while obtaining close to 14 miles per gallon. The average car is driven 220 miles per week.[2,3] Reducing gasoline consumption by two million barrels per day would mean a 25 percent reduction in driving—the average car could be driven only 155 miles per week. That would not be a trivial reduction, but neither would it be an insurmountable loss if carpooling and more careful trip planning were used to absorb the loss. The routes to work and stores could remain open, and prudence would result in gasoline left over for recreation and vacations.

Table 2

Vehicle Miles Traveled by
Trip Purpose and Household Income

Trip Purpose	Annual Household Income			
	Under $4000	$4000-$9999	$10000-$14999	$15000 & Over
	Percent of Vehicle-Miles Traveled			
Earning a Living	31.0	39.6	44.0	47.4
Family Business	27.1	20.0	18.0	17.0
Education, Civic and Religious	4.4	4.9	5.3	5.5
Social and Recreational	35.7	34.2	31.5	28.9
Other	1.8	1.3	1.2	1.2
Total, All Purposes	100.0	100.0	100.0	100.0

Source: Note 6

The issue of equity becomes apparent here. Gasoline consumption per household varies by income, primarily because automobile ownership is largely determined by income. Table 4 illustrates this fact, showing that families with an average income of less than $3,000 (1974 dollars) owned an average of 0.5 cars, while families with an average income of $10,000 to $12,000 (1974 dollars) owned an average of 1.5 cars. Only 38 percent of the families in the former category owned at least one car, while more than 90 percent of the families in the latter category owned at least one car.[2] This disparity is a central issue in the debate over the merits of gasoline rationing, taxation, and other controls. While poorer people may drive their cars as many miles per year as wealthier persons, they own fewer cars and therefore do less driving. Such issues must be carefully considered in the formulation of any gasoline reduction policy it if is to succeed.

Table 3

Vehicle Ownership in the United States by Family Income
and Family Size, 1974

	Number of Families	Average No. of Vehicles Owned	Percent Owning at Least One Vehicle
	(millions)	(millions)	
Family Income Before Taxes (1974)			
Under $3,000	10.3	.5	38%
$3,000 to $3,999	3.9	.7	57
$4,000 to $4,999	3.7	.9	71
$5,000 to $5,999	3.4	1.0	80
$6,000 to $6,999	3.6	1.2	83
$7,000 to $7,999	3.3	1.2	87
$8,000 to $9,999	6.5	1.4	91
$10,000 to $11,999 ...	6.5	1.5	94
$12,000 to $14,999 ...	7.7	1.7	96
$15,000 to $19,999 ...	7.8	1.8	97
$20,000 to $24,999 ...	3.5	2.0	98
$25,000 and Over	3.4	2.1	98
Not Reported	8.3	1.2	72
Family Size			
1 Person	17.0	.6	53%
2 Persons	20.4	1.2	84
3 Persons	11.6	1.5	87
4 Persons	10.5	1.7	91
5 Persons	6.4	1.8	92
6 Persons or More	5.8	1.7	88

Source: Note 2

1.3 When Should this Reduction be Achieved?

Over the next 15-20 years it could be possible to cut automobile
consumption of gasoline by three million barrels per day without any curtailment of automotive use. (This calculation assumes an increase in vehicle miles traveled per year from 10,000
to 12,000, and an increase in registered automobiles from 120
million to 150 million by the year 2000.) This cut in consumption could be accomplished by producing a fleet of cars which
obtain an average of 37 miles per gallon, a goal which is techni-

cally and economically feasible. Such an improvement would represent the essence of conservation—the economic increase in energy productivity to provide a given level of services or amenity.

Time is required for conservation, based on a shift in the composition of the auto fleet to much more efficient vehicles. Meanwhile, the United States currently faces the prospect of an oil shortage of crisis proportions. Assuming that the best target for reducing United States oil imports is to reduce its gasoline consumption, and that an appropriate level of reduction equals 2 million barrels per day, we may ask, "What are the best means of effecting such a reduction?" We recognize that no option is entirely satisfactory, and that it is important to avoid foreclosing long-term energy conservation options with the choices made for short-term relief. With these caveats, we may proceed to evaluate the various policy tools available.

2. Specific Policy Tools for Reducing Gasoline Consumption

There are many policy tools which could be applied to reduce United States gasoline consumption with relative immediacy. These include:

1. Free Market Pricing
2. Gasoline Lines, Weekend Service Station Closings, No-Drive Days, Odd/Even Fill-ups, Running-out, etc.
3. Oil Import Fees or Quotas
4. Gasoline Rationing
5. Gasoline Taxation
6. Rapid Transit, Van Pooling, Diamond Lanes, etc.

These tools, individually and in combination, must be evaluated for effectiveness, equity, manageability, and inflationary effect.

2.1 Free Market Pricing

The price mechanism presently controls how most goods in the United States are allocated. Recent developments in the energy market can be used to argue against non-market controls on energy, i.e., that the price mechanism is functioning as it should. Demand for gasoline, with the price ranging between $1.10 and $1.50 per gallon,[4] is down 10 percent compared to 1979 (over the four-week period ending January 4, 1980). Compared to the average demand from 1975-1979 (for the same four-week period), demand is down five percent.[5] Gasoline prices jumped 8.5 percent in February, and are 75 percent higher relative to 1979.[4] If gasoline reaches $2.00 per gallon in 1981, demand will be further diminished. Although market pricing has been held to be ineffective in the short run, inequitable, and inflationary, it is the least cumbersome of the consumption reduction tools to administer, and possibly the fairest in the long run.

Energy is price-inelastic* in the short term, though it is less so over longer periods. Recent experience with price increases as well as results from cross-sectional statistical analysis indicates a price-inelasticity of approximately −0.15 for gasoline within a period of four months, with a higher rate—perhaps −0.4—over periods of a year.[6]

Many object strongly to what they perceive as the inequality of the price mechanism. It forces poor people to pay a disproportionate share of their incomes for what has become a necessity of modern life. The inflationary effect of rising prices compounds this inequity since the poor suffer most from inflation. Whether these equity issues are strong enough to counter the argument that pricing energy below its market value encourages its waste—to the profound detriment of human health, the natural environment, and national security—will remain a hotly debated question.

2.2 Oil Import Fees or Quotas

The most positive aspects of imposing either import fees or quotas are their direct application and political expediency. That is, the importation of foreign crude oil can be discouraged directly and quickly by the imposition of a fee or a limitation of the total permissible volume of imports. The President presently has authority under the Federal Trade Expansion Act of 1962 to enact either of those actions. Mr. Carter recently imposed a $4.62 per barrel fee on imported oil. The fee would be passed through to consumers only in the form of a 10¢ per gallon gasoline tax. This action is being challenged in the courts, primarily by gasoline wholesalers, who maintain that the principal effect of the fee would be to increase carrying charges for their inventory. They say that the plan would work only with the cooperation of all distributors, and is unlikely to be effective. Some would argue that these difficulties are severe enough to discount import fees or quotas as suitable methods for achieving reduction in gasoline consumption.

---

*Price inelasticity is the percent reduction in demand in response to a one percent increase in price. A zero percent response is defined as perfectly inelastic demand. Demand response ranging between zero and −1.0 is defined as inelastic, while a response greater than −1.0 is defined as elastic.

2.3 Weekend Station Closings, Gasoline Lines, Odd/Even Plans, No-Drive Days, etc.

Weekend gasoline station closings, as a means of reducing gasoline consumption, has been described as "the Sword of Damocles."[7] This method has been frowned upon both by Congress and a large number of state governments who depend heavily on the tourist industry for revenues.[8] While weekend closings are effective—they do reduce consumption—they place a disproportionate burden on the tourist industry. This is considered inequitable, as well as undesirable for travelers.

One might conclude—judging from recent history—that gasoline lines are an unacceptable method of curbing gasoline demand: people have been killed in them.

A number of other gasoline curtailment options can be imagined. Allowing motorists to fill their tanks only on even- or odd-numbered days, depending upon the motorists' license plate, is a measure which probably does little to curtail gasoline consumption since the average motorist fills his or her tank only once every five to ten days. But this measure might help minimize the length—and the violence—of gasoline lines during a crisis.

"No drive days" is a concept in which each motorist would choose one day per week to leave his or her car at home. A car sticker would designate this choice, and would make the use of the car illegal on that day of the week. While the idea is idealistic in that it would allow choice in curtailment, it perhaps requires an unrealistic amount of planning on the part of motorists, and for that and other reasons is probably unenforceable. Most would argue that curtailment is less desirable than conservation.

Unpalatable alternatives such as the above, however, would be the only options available if the United States supply of foreign oil were to be suddenly truncated. For this reason, an emergency standby gasoline allocated system is being readied by the Department of Energy.

2.4 Gasoline Rationing

Gasoline rationing should have one distinct advantage: it might be effective. The government could determine in advance what volume of gasoline would be available for national consumption and set the level by allocating the corresponding quantity of entitlements. But the difficulty and potential unfairness in the allocation of entitlements, or ration rights, are rationing's major drawbacks.

There are many possible ways to ration gasoline. One can envision a modern system that would work electronically with bank-card type ration rights facilitating inexpensive, computerized keeping of complex ration records. Such a system would require a number of years to develop, however, leaving only coupon-based systems as an alternative in the interim.

2.4.a *The World War II Experience with Rationing*
In 1940, there were 25 million cars in the United States. Each vehicle traveled an average 9000 miles per year, and obtained about 15 miles per gallon. Annual consumption of gasoline averaged 600 gallons, or about 12 gallons per week.[2] Rationing during the war reduced total demand for gasoline by about 35 percent.[9]

Fixed-value, non-negotiable gasoline ration coupons were distributed during the war on the basis of need. From 1942 to 1944, gasoline was rationed in three categories of allotments:
1. Category A: Low-priority users—four gallons per week.
2. Category B: Users who drove to work—nine gallons per week.
3. Category C: Doctors, firemen, etc.—unlimited allotments.

Local boards were created to determine who would get each allotment, and each car was labeled by category and matched with a coupon book to be carried only with that car.

A black market for coupons did develop. Over a two-year period, for example, there were 2000 criminal convictions for black marketing, 4000 service stations lost their licenses for the same crime, and 32,500 motorists lost their ration books for violations. Because of abuses, after only two years an entirely new set of entitlements had to be created to replace the original set.[9]

Significantly, World War II was a time when the urgency of gasoline rationing was undeniable. Given the justifiable fear of a black market, the difficulty of fairly ascertaining need, the much greater base demand for gasoline today, and general skepticism about the reality of the 'energy crisis', the provision of a white-market mechanism for the redistribution of ration entitlements appears to be reasonable.

2.4.b *Standby Gasoline Rationing: the Proposed DOE Plan*
The Energy Policy and Conservation Act of 1975 (EPCA)[10] provides authority for the President to devise a standby motor fuels rationing plan. Such a plan was presented to Congress by the Carter Administration in March 1979. The plan was approved by the Senate, but was rejected by the House of Representatives on

March 10. Subsequently, on November 5, the Emergency Energy Conservation Act was enacted.[11] This act amended EPCA by changing the approval and implementation processes for a rationing plan. It requires that the President submit a standby gasoline and diesel fuel rationing plan for Congressional approval "as soon as practicable," and that the plan may be considered approved unless a joint resolution of disapproval is passed within 30 days after the plan is submitted. The President may veto the resolution of disapproval, and thereby enact the plan if either house fails to override the veto with a two-thirds majority.

The plan, after approval, would "go onto a shelf" until needed. It could be implemented only after the President determined that either a 20 percent shortage of gasoline, fuel oil, or diesel fuel had existed for more than 30 days, or that the nation's health, economy, or safety were threatened. In the former case, either house of Congress could disapprove implementation within 15 days of the President's request; in the latter case, implementation could only occur with approval of both houses within 30 days, and authority for this implementation would expire after 60 days.

The Department of Energy has drafted such a plan, but at the time of this writing had not submitted it to Congress. The basic elements of this plan are known from a notice of proposed rulemaking published in the Federal Register,[12] and through interviews with administration sources.[13]

If implementation of the standby rationing plan were approved by Congress, the administration would initiate gasoline rationing in the following steps:

1. DOE would determine the available national supply of gasoline.
2. States would be allotted a share of ration rights based on historical consumption, minus an amount held for a National Ration Reserve.
3. DOE would determine the quantity of entitlements to be given firms, farmers, and other priority class activities and persons within each state.
4. Individual shares of each state's allotment would be determined for private use by dividing each state's share (minus the priority allocation and an amount which will be held as a State Ration Reserve) by the number of licensed private vehicles in that state.
5. Entitlement checks which would be redeemable for coupons would be mailed to each qualifying party.

6. The entitlement checks for coupons could be cashed at banks or other participating institutions. Savings accounts for coupons would be made available.
7. Ration Boards would be established for hardship cases, appeals, etc.
8. Coupons, in five gallon denominations, would be presented for purchase with the purchase price of gasoline to gasoline station operators. Operators could, however, sell gasoline without receiving coupons, provided that he or she obtained on the open market an amount of coupons equal to the amount of gasoline sold in order to 'pay' the wholesaler.
9. Coupons could be bought and/or sold at banks, gasoline stations, department stores, or any participating institution.
10. DOE could buy and sell coupons in order to regulate the coupon market.

The problems inherent in rationing are obvious in this plan. Allocation on the basis of automobile ownership is bitterly contested by many who prefer allocation on a per capita basis. These people see per car allocation as basically inequitable and discriminating against the poor as well as those who use alternate means of transportation, own no car, but still have gasoline requirements.

The distribution of the coupons themselves is a major problem since coupons cannot be mailed directly to individuals. Being negotiable and of considerable value, coupons could be stolen from mailboxes. This problem, moreover, is indicative of a larger, more basic difficulty, that of managing what essentially would become a second currency.

Further, determining the rights of firms, special consumer categories, and others will be difficult and expensive. DOE recently estimated that pre-implementation costs will total $300 million. Implementation of the full rationing plan itself might cost $2 to $4 billion per year.[13,14] At this writing, the DOE plan remains amorphous; with uncertainty remaining as to how the rationing plan might actually work, even DOE employees are conceding that it might not work at all. Beyond these difficulties, a plan for the rationing of diesel will not be prepared until after a gasoline rationing plan is approved.

2.4.c *The Manageability of Rationing*
The management difficulties and the cost of coupon rationing are evident in the sheer magnitude of the system that would be required. The United States consumes about 9 billion gallons of

gasoline per month. DOE has estimated that a 20 percent gasoline shortage would result in a coupon white market value of between $1 and $2 per gallon. The entitlement coupons placed into circulation each month would be worth between $7 and $14 billion: the number of coupons would be greater than the number of all the United States treasury notes in circulation.

The banking industry has estimated that the negotiation of coupons would require an additional 150,000 tellers, 50 percent more than the banking industry now employs, if banks alone handle the transactions. This estimate was based on the assumption that persons would receive checks for coupons in the mail, wish to redeem them within one week, arrive at the bank windows at a completely uniform rate, and could be served within two minutes.[7] This problem could be reduced, of course, by using institutions other than banks for coupon redemption and staggered mailings of checks. Additional employees would be required to serve on the special, local ration boards.

Coupon rationing might also cause problems for independent gasoline retailers. Some believe that major oil companies could, with their discretionary income, purchase large quantities of coupons in order to make them available at their retail outlets. Independent, less wealthy dealers would be disadvantaged when coupon seekers were attracted by the availability of coupons for purchase at major companies' stations.

It is not clear what would happen to price controls under rationing. Nothing in the gasoline rationing plan would end gasoline price controls before their scheduled demise on September 30, 1981. Price controls would not be needed, theoretically, if rationing worked well. But if too many coupons were printed, or if counterfeiting were widespread, price controls might be deemed necessary.

2.4.d Rationing and Equity

The problem of wealthier interests controlling coupon availability recalls the question of eligibility of ration rights. On which basis should entitlements be allocated: per car or per capita?

Per capita rationing would require distribution of entitlements according to some form of identification such as driver's licenses, social security numbers, voter registration cards, or some special number or piece of identification. Of course, not all people have each of these pieces of identification, and some object that standardizing an old identity system—or creating a new, national system—heightens the risk of abuse of civil liberties.

Basing allocation on driver's licenses is frequently proposed as a surrogate for per capita distribution. Congress, in fact, required in the EECA that DOE pay special attention to this option. There is no substantial economic impediment to obtaining a license, and therefore future ration rights—as there is to purchasing a car. States which prefer allocation based on driver's licenses do so primarily for that economic reason, but also because a larger segment of the population—134 million people—would be included.* Still, 26 million adult Americans who do not possess driver's licenses would either be left out by this method or would be motivated to obtain licenses simply to be able to receive and sell coupons. More seriously, some citizens—it is not known how many—have licenses from several states. Since few states use Social Security numbers or any common number which could be checked from state to state to reduce fraud, there seems to be little reason to expect that the practice of obtaining many licenses and thus too many coupons could be prevented.[12]

If car ownership were based on real need, some argue, then per car rationing would be the more equitable rationing system since those who have cars will be those who need gasoline. Many states favor this approach because under their existing registration systems they believe it to be easier to manage and check for fraud.[8] There is, however, definitely a higher rate of car ownership among higher income groups (See Table 2), and junk yards might rapidly be emptied as clunkers were purchased by persons seeking to increase their coupon receipts. Limiting the number of cars eligible for ration rights per household (with hardship cases having resort to a ration appeals board) would minimize this dilemma.

Proponents of rationing on a per car basis note that under either distribution system, the poor would be net sellers of coupons. Low income families would benefit more greatly from a license-based plan, but the burden this redistribution of income would impose on middle- and upper-income families— who would be net purchasers—is unacceptable to some. The difference in magnitude of the potential income redistribution is shown in Table 4. This table, prepared by DOE, shows that low-income persons would be favored with a net income gain under either plan.[12]

---

*A total of 160 million adult Americans are eligible to obtain driver's licenses.

Table 4

Equity and Gasoline Ration Rights Allocation—
Driver's License vs. Vehicle Registration

Average Household Annual Net Value
of Allotment Sales (Purchases)
(Based on 1977 dollars)

Household Disposable Income	Vehicle Based Plan	License Based Plan
Under $5,000	$107	$303
5,000 - 9,999	+ 63	+163
10,000 - 14,999	- 26	- 52
15,000 - 19,999	- 43	-132
20,000 - 24,999	-102	-248
25,000 - 29,999	-104	-269
30,000 or more	- 63	-267

2.4.e *Rationing, in Summary*

The DOE plan—supplemented by restrictions on eligible cars per household—might indeed be the least noxious of the alternative rationing plans. Distribution of ration coupons on a per car basis might well be more manageable than on a per driver's license basis since fraud would be less likely. It is useful to remember, however, that none of the rationing systems is without major flaws, and that although DOE claims it could have a rationing system in place within six weeks in the event of an emergency, rationing might only replace gasoline lines with coupon lines. A smooth-running system (by DOE's own estimates) would take 12-18 months to implement. Rationing would not be an overnight success.

Moreover, for rationing to work, many argue that a great degree of national cohesion would be required. This might arise only in the most urgent of emergencies. Inequities in coupon allocation, as well as fraud and administrative bungling, will surely be matters of public scrutiny. Rationing, therefore, with all its administrative and equity problems, may be a policy tool that would work only in a time of emergency, limited by the public's perception of inequity and administrative ineptitude. The end of rationing would, in any event, signal the end of the crisis, and might spur the resumption of prior consumption patterns.

2.5 Gasoline Taxation

Common wisdom has it that everyone resists taxation. Yet as the United States becomes more wary of its dependence on foreign oil, the clamor attendant on gasoline tax proposals grows.

Like rationing, a tax could be made effective. Some estimates of price elasticity indicate that if gasoline prices were doubled by taxation over the present level of $1.10 to $1.50 per gallon, then total gasoline demand might fall between 10 and 20 percent, or between 700,000 and 1.4 million barrels of oil per day. Some say that a two million barrel per day demand reduction (from gasoline consumption alone) might require a gasoline tax of $2 or more per gallon.

Others, however, point out that there is not sufficient experience on which to base a reasonably accurate assessment of demand elasticity in the present environment. They argue that a smaller gas tax, clearly proclaimed as aimed at conservation and combined with other measures, might bring a two million barrel a day reduction.

The administrative mechanisms for dealing with a gasoline tax are already in place, making a tax much more manageable than rationing. That is, the tax can readily be collected, and rebating the revenues can be accomplished through the federal income tax system, the Social Security system, or others. What is done with tax revenues, however, determines the equity of gasoline taxation relative to rationing.

Several tax rebate schemes have been proposed. Some would tax gasoline moderately, with revenues going to offset other taxes or to finance energy conservation. Others propose a much stiffer tax, but call for the distribution of tax exemption coupons to be issued for a minimum amount of individual need. Direct tax rebate methods have been detailed, as have systems for rebating the tax revenues to the states which would then determine their use or means of rebate.

2.5.a *John Anderson/Bennett Johnston Proposals*

Congressman John Anderson has proposed a 50 cents per gallon "motor fuels conservation tax," applying to both gasoline and diesel fuel, which he would couple with a 50 percent reduction in Social Security taxes and a compensatory hike in Social Security benefits for the elderly and disabled. Rep. Anderson estimates that such a tax would generate $55 billion annually and conserve .7 million barrels of oil per day, or eight percent of United States oil imports.

Anderson's tax might cause a 2.4 percent increase in the Consumer Price Index, but the rebate would offset the decline in purchasing power. Under Anderson's plan, a person with a gross income of $6,200 per year would receive a payroll tax deduction of $194. By using less than 388 gallons of gasoline in that year, the individual would enjoy a net tax benefit. A family with an income of $20,000 per year would receive $626 in payroll tax relief, allowing the use of 1252 gallons per year with a net tax benefit. Social Security benefits would increase so that use of 20 gallons or less per month by Social Security recipients would result in a net benefit to them; workers not contributing to Social Security would receive income tax credits.

Families with incomes of less than $8,000 a year travel, on the average, less than 5,000 vehicle miles per year. Anderson's proposal would give them a tax benefit if they drive less than 5,720 miles per year. As with rationing, there would be a slight redistribution of income toward low-income groups, if past driving patterns were maintained. Higher income groups would pay more for their driving privileges, and would thus be given incentives to conserve.[15] In other words, the Anderson proposal slightly favors lower-income groups.

Senator Bennett Johnston has proposed a similar tax in the Senate. During the fall of 1979 he introduced legislation which would impose a 50 cent tax on a gallon of gasoline. Revenues would be rebated either to the states to offset sales taxes, or through the Social Security system.[16]

2.5.b *The Galbraith/UAW Approach*
John Kenneth Galbraith[17] and the United Auto Workers (UAW)[18] have separately proposed a large gasoline tax. Tax exemption coupons—or energy stamps—would be issued to all consumers at an equal per capita rate, based on a predetermined level of need. This combination of taxation and rationing would provide an immediate and powerful incentive to conserve while minimizing the financial burden on the poor.

The problem with these plans is that they both involve coupons. The difficulties that cause some to fear rationing are identical in a tax-exemption coupon system. This observation has led some to advocate "green coupon" rebates; that is, the direct rebate of a gasoline tax with money (or checks).

2.5.c *A Direct Rebate Proposal*
Noting that the purpose of a gasoline tax is to reduce gasoline consumption and not to raise revenues, Robert Williams of

Princeton University has proposed a stiff gasoline tax of $2 per gallon which would be rebated directly to each adult. A $2 tax would raise about $150 billion in the first year, which would mean that all persons 16 years old and older could receive a check for $730 per year, regardless of the amount of gasoline consumed.* Obviously, the more gasoline an individual used, the greater penalty he or she would pay. One who consumed no gasoline would increase his or her income by $730 per year. An average family could "break even" with the tax by reducing household gasoline consumption by 25 percent (from more than 1000 gallons to 770). According to Williams, such a reduction could be achieved either by driving less or by using a more fuel efficient car. A typical household driving an average 14,000 miles per year could "break even" by using a car obtaining 19 miles per gallon. Commercial users would receive rebates through corporate income tax reductions.

An interesting effect of this plan is that the net income of poor families, who drive less on the average, would increase. Increased mobility would result because mobility is income-elastic. Thus, while middle- and upper-income groups decreased their gasoline consumption, primarily by reducing discretionary driving, lower income groups would actually in-crease consumption and attain a higher standard of living. This outcome contrasts markedly with other scenarios of reduction of gasoline consumption.[19]

One major difficulty of this program is that poor people would be hurt by cash flow problems if the rebate came only at the end of every year. For this reason, individuals below certain income levels would need to receive "pre-bates," or at least regular, early rebates.

2.5.d Tax Rebates to the States

Clark Bullard[20] has proposed a rebate system which would allow states to determine how revenues were rebated. Impor-tantly, this plan would provide incentives to states for meeting energy conservation targets, targets which the President may set pursuant to EECA.†

---

*Checks would be distributed through the income tax system. Those who do not ordinarily file income tax returns could do so easily in order to receive the rebate.

†The President is authorized to set state energy conservation targets if he determines that a national energy emergency exists. The targets are based on a uniform percentage reduction for all states using historic consumption data for each state, adjusted for demand growth, weather,

Under Bullard's plan, the federal tax would be increased initially by $.50 per gallon, and would rise to $1 to $2 per gallon by 1990. The revenues would be rebated to the governor of each state, who would be responsible for distributing the rebates among individuals in any manner that state determined to be fair. The federal government would distribute half the revenues among the states on a simple per capita basis, while the other half would be distributed proportional to each state's success in reducing gasoline usage per capita.

Most proposals for equitably distributing ration coupons or gasoline tax revenues are based on data collected and maintained by states (that is driver's licenses, registered vehicles). A state would be free to select whatever scheme it perceived to be most equitable. The Federal Government might offer to assist states who choose a per capita rebate plan, by using income tax and social security records. Commercial consumers would receive rebates through the federal corporate income tax system.

By providing incentives, the federal tax would reward actions by state and local governments that changed the institutional structure within which consumers meet conservation opportunities. The operating efficiency of transportation systems, for example, can be increased by better regulations such as priority treatment for car pools and buses, so that mass-transit travel times are faster than for single-occupant automobiles, or by road-pricing schemes such as Singapore's. States might change laws such as taxi regulation, insurance liability, etc., which discourage ridesharing. Such actions would facilitate an immediate but nevertheless long-lasting reduction in gasoline consumption, effectively increasing the price elasticity of gasoline demand.

3. Summary

We have reviewed the merits and demerits of a number of proposed policies for reducing gasoline consumption in the United States. We observed that the United States could face major political and strategic problems concerning Middle Eastern oil, including the possibility of a direct confrontation with the USSR over Middle East oil resources. We have also observed that the United States stands little prepared to reduce its dependence

---

or other factors. Each governor is required to submit within 45 days after notification by the President a plan for meeting the emergency reduction targets. The Secretary of Energy must approve or disapprove of this plan within 30 days.

on foreign oil supplies. The policies for reducing gasoline consumption were examined for their potential effectiveness, manageability, equity, and inflationary impact. We dwelled largely on gasoline rationing and taxation, believing that these tools offer the greatest potential, although we noted that the price mechanism is working and can be credited with a five to ten percent reduction in gasoline demand. We focused on gasoline consumption primarily because it is such a large fraction of total petroleum use in the United States: 7 million barrels of gasoline are consumed in this country each day. This is on the same scale as US oil imports—8 to 8.5 million barrels per day.

We suggest that it might be appropriate for the United States to further reduce its demand for oil by two million barrels per day. This is an amount equal to the daily United States oil imports via the vulnerable Strait of Hormuz. The reduction of gasoline demand by two million barrels per day would diminish inflation by reducing the pressure for oil price increases, would increase the United States' flexibility in foreign policy, and might help avert a major military confrontation. The reduction in gasoline consumption would reduce the mobility of the average private vehicle from 220 to 155 miles per week, or 25 percent.

The best strategy over the long run, we believe, is to increase the energy productivity of automobiles. Achieving fuel economies of 40 miles per gallon in new cars on the road in the early 1990s should be a top national priority.

Interim curtailment measures are necessary, nonetheless. A standby gasoline rationing plan is required, although we believe that the proposed Department of Energy plan may work poorly if implemented. This is due to a lack of specific mechanisms for facilitating the allocation, distribution, and negotiation of ration rights. Equity issues will continue to be divisive, pitting those who would protect the mobility of poor people and non-car owners against those who would allocate ration rights on the basis of need as perceived in terms of car ownership. We conclude that the proposed standby gasoline rationing plan should not be implemented except in the event of an urgent national emergency.

A rationing plan could be devised to work, especially with the use of computers. But such a system would take years to develop, and national needs in the United States are more demanding. A gasoline tax, fortunately, could be made to be effective, equitable, and would in any event be manageable.

A significant gasoline tax could reduce consumption significantly, moving toward the target of a two million barrel per day reduction. Such a tax would generate enormous revenues. These should be either rebated directly to all adults on an equal basis through the federal income tax system or directly to the states. "Prebates" could be made available for low income persons in order to eliminate the cash flow problems such a tax would create, and rebates for commercial vehicles could be made through the federal corporate income tax system. In the latter case, the states would determine how the revenues would be rebated. Further, the amount of revenues returned to each state could be based on a combination of rebates on a per capita basis, and on the basis of how successful each state was in achieving certain energy conservation targets. In any case, a gasoline tax could be made as effective and as equitable as any gasoline rationing system, and would be far more manageable.

1. Estimate derived from "International Energy Statistical Review" and Department of Energy data.

2. "MVMA Motor Vehicle Facts and Figures '79," Motor Vehicle Manufacturers Association of the United States, Inc., Detroit, Michigan.

3. "Monthly Energy Review," October, 1979, US Department of Energy, Energy Information Administration, Washington, D.C.

4. John T. McQuistan, "Gas at the Pump is Nearly $1.50," New York Times, March 3, 1980; William K. Stevens, "Liters (Amid Confusion) Replace Gallons at Houston Pumps," New York Times, March 4, 1980; John R. Emshwiller and Peter B. Roche, "Throttling Down? Motorists Have Curbed Appetite for Gasoline in US, Analysts Say," Wall Street Journal, March 6, 1980; Jonathan Fuerbringer, "Producer Prices Up Again; Energy Leads the Way," Washington Star, March 7, 1980.

5. "Weekly Petroleum Status Report," February 22, 1980, US Department of Energy, Energy Information Administration, Washington, D.C.

6. "The Automobile Sector: A Preliminary Energy Conservation Strategy Assessment," March 30, 1979, US Department of Energy, Office of Conservation and Advanced Systems Policy, Office of the Assistant Secretary for Policy and Evaluation, Washington, D.C.

7. "Mandatory Energy Conservation and Gasoline and Diesel Fuel Rationing," Hearings before the Subcommittee on Energy Regulation of the Committee on Energy and Natural Resources, US Senate, 96th Congress, March 19 and 20, 1979.

8. Hearings Records of the US Department of Energy, Economic Regulatory Administration, Hearings on the Proposed Standby Gasoline Rationing Program, January, 1980, Washington, D.C.

9. Michael Mossetig, personal communication regarding research in progress, February 1980.

10. Energy Policy and Conservation Act of 1975, P.L. 94-163.

11. Emergency Energy Conservation Act of 1979, P.L. 96-102.

12. Federal Register, Volume 44, No. 238, Monday, December 10, 1979, Proposed Rules, 70799.

13. Personal Communication, Bill Strauss, Interagency Task Force on Gasoline Rationing, March, 1980.

14. Hazel Rollins, US Department of Energy, Economic Regulatory Administration, Testimony before the Subcommittee on Energy Regulation of the Committee on Energy and Natural Resources, US Senate, 96th Congress, January 28, 1980.

15. Rep. John Anderson, "Questions and Answers Regarding the Anderson Proposal," January 1980, Washington, D.C.

16. Congressional Quarterly, February 23, 1980, Washington, D.C.

17. John Kenneth Galbraith, "Oil: A Modest Proposal," The New York Review of Books, Volume XXVI, Number 14, September 27, 1979.

18. Howard Young, "UAW Statement to US DOE Request for Comment on Changes in Retail Gasoline Price Regulation (Docket No. ERA-R-7932), International Union, United Auto Workers, July 11, 1979.

19. Robert H. Williams, "A $2 a Gallon Political Opportunity," in this volume. Energy and Environmental Studies, Princeton University, February 19, 1980.

20. Clark Bullard, US Congress Office of Technology Assessment, Personal Communication, February-March, 1980. Washington, D.C.

ALTERNATIVES FOR GASOLINE
by Thomas C. Schelling

There are three generic alternatives to a free market in gasoline that are receiving attention. One is called "allocation," and directs supplies up to some point short of the consumer. A second is called "rationing," and sets quantities that the consumer may purchase. The third is taxation.

We have had federal allocations by state, using the regular distribution system up to the retailer, with some allowances for preferred users like emergency vehicles. In the absence of price controls, an allocation system redistributes consumers among retailers, can lead to price differences between states, and might somewhat redistribute the proceeds within the network of distribution. Coupled with effective price controls, an allocation system will lead to visible "shortages," i.e., excess demand at the controlled price, unless enough specific restrictions on driving are simultaneously imposed to reduce demand, state by state if necessary, for the available supply. Without such restrictions there is bound to occur some kind of "informal rationing," through gas lines, favoritism, illicit bartering and illicit pricing, and changed driving habits due to the uncertainties and the vagaries as well as the quantities of supply. Hoarding is then attractive to people who have any place—including fuller gas tanks—to keep gasoline without too great a fire hazard.

"Rationing" was universal in World War II. Gasoline shortages, it should be remembered, were then associated with shortages of tires, spare parts, and new vehicles. At that time foods, leather goods, and other commodities were rationed; rents and housing were controlled, and labor was allocated. The gas rations were allocated to registered *vehicles*; but vehicle *use*, including daily distance to work, determined the ration category of the vehicle. For gasoline, as for shoes and milk, there were local ration boards to which one could appeal one's ration assignment.

A crucial feature of wartime rationing was that any transfer of gasoline or coupons was a federal offense. There was no legal market in coupons. Mere possession of coupons not registered in one's name was an offense, and counterfeit coupons could not be explained away. Enforcement was not bad; "excess" driving was conspicuous, penalties were severe, and of course, there was a war on.

Taxes, the third "system," can be of several kinds that work differently (aside from what may be done with the proceeds).

Thomas C. Schelling is Littauer Professor of Political Economy at Harvard University's Kennedy School of Government, where he is Chairman of the Program in Public Administration. He is the author of a number of books, including *Thinking through the Energy Problem, Micromotive and Macrobehavior,* and *International Economics.*

The familiar gasoline tax is a "specific duty," a tax on gallons, not on money value. A tax can be on the value of the sale ("ad valorem"), varying with the price. Ad valorem duties are common but not on gasoline. Finally, a relevant tax when the purpose is to moderate demand or to capture a "windfall," is an "incremental ad valorem tax." That would be a tax proportionate to the excess of the price per gallon above some base price. (With a base price set at $1.25 and a 75 percent incremental tax rate, a gallon sold for $1.65 would be taxed at 30¢.)

Because stations sell two or three grades of gasoline and some are self-service, and because prices differ from region to region or from locality to locality, a tax on the price increment may entail base-price differentials.

Because gasoline is distributed through regulated pumps that display the transactions visibly, and are already subject to both federal and state taxation and EPA regulation, none of these taxes pose any problem of collection. Economic reasoning leads to the conclusion that it makes no difference whether the tax is nominally levied against ("paid by") the consumer or the retailer. There might be some difference in the consumer's perception of the relation between tax and price under the different tax schemes; if a 30-cent tax appears to be "added on" as part of a $1.65 price, consumers might suppose that without the tax the price could have been $1.35, while a tax that appears to take 30¢ of the retailer's 40-cent excess over the base price might be seen as "capturing a windfall." The question whether consumers would see it that way is different from the question whether that's the "right way" to look at it.

Having identified allocations, rations, and taxes as the relevant alternative "systems," it remains to analyze rationing and taxation as alternatives to the allocation system that nominally still obtains. The analysis will first examine the main alternative forms of rationing and then compare them with taxation to see how they work on gasoline demand and how they compare in the distribution of benefits and hardships, in equity, and the appearance of equity.

First, there is a point about a "non-system." There are many regulations that attempt to reduce the demand for gasoline by means other than operating on gasoline sales. These include fleet-mileage standards for auto producers, speed limits, fast lanes or reduced bridge tolls for cars with several occupants, subsidies to public transportation, and restrictions on the days that people can drive or the days they can buy gasoline, the locations in which people may drive, even the vehicles that may be driven at certain times and places. Unlike rationing, these restrictions typically do not add up to a "system." They collectively contain no mechanism that assures a quantitative outcome. Rationing necessarily imposes some collective ceiling on the purchase of gasoline. Special demand-reducing taxation would be oriented toward some estimated point on a demand curve. A ban on Sunday driving is more opportunistic. This does not mean that in the aggregate a collection of specific restrictions could not be of sufficient severity of impact to reduce gasoline use substantially, even to the quantity that a rationing scheme would impose. But it is unlikely that a major programmed reduction in gasoline use would be implemented by specific restrictions that were not coupled to a rationing or a taxing system.

Rationing: The Main Alternatives

Although one might prefer to ration miles driven, or passenger miles, or some weighted average of different kinds of miles, what is going to be rationed if we have rationing is gasoline. More accurately, motor vehicle fuel, including diesel, probably with no quantitative distinction between leaded and unleaded. There will probably be no rationing of tires or anything else related to driving. There may be separate rationing systems or unlimited fuel for certain vehicles or certain purposes or certain vehicle owners—farm vehicles, taxis, buses, trucks, fire and police and telephone company and military vehicles, fishing boats, construction vehicles, industrial fork-lift and other trucks, delivery vehicles, or still others. This could involve a significant portion of the motor fuels. There may be special arrangements for private companies that institute passenger service to and from work, possibly through the pooling or partial pooling of rations by employees. The share of the motor fuel covered by a rationing system might be somewhere between two-thirds and nine-tenths.

Many issues will be wrapped up in the handling of all of those "special" vehicles and uses just mentioned. Ideal inclusions and exclusions will be administratively infeasible, either to determine in principle or in enforcement—for instance, it will be very difficult to ensure that the farmer does not use part of his truck or tractor ration in driving the family car to town. An important point to keep in mind is that the decisions whether or not to *tax* the fuels used by farmers, cab drivers, and delivery services may be less consequential, i.e., easier to decide or to compromise, than inclusions and exclusions in a *rationing* scheme.

A key characteristic of any rationing scheme is its basis, i.e., who or what qualifies for a ration. Among the bases usually considered, somewhat in order of likely adoption, are: registered vehicles (perhaps requiring a registration date prior to some cutoff), licensed drivers, families with a registered vehicle and at least one licensed driver, and some more inclusive population set, such as adults. The basis will depend somewhat on other features of the system. Marketable coupons, for example, being disposable for cash could be distributed more widely without the anomaly of coupons being unusable by people who momentarily had neither car nor driver's license. "Family" is, of course, hard to define. As with the "man in the house" criterion for welfare, a definition of family could affect living arrangements—e.g., teen-agers living at home or not—if the gas or the coupons were worth it. Probably new driver's licenses would qualify but not newly-registered antique vehicles. There would have to be some kind of national registration, and all residents who preferred to go "undocumented" would not qualify. (For many reasons, including counterfeit problems, any rationing system will be centralized in the federal government.)

Just to have rough orders of magnitude: the average passenger car burns 750 gallons a year, or 15 gallons per week. Because a significant portion will be in categories that are unrationed or get extra rations, the round number of 10 gallons per week that shows up in discussion of rationing is not a bad round number to have in mind. Keep in mind that "rural" driving entails many more miles per vehicle than urban, the difference being twofold. Miles per car vary between areas like Los Angeles, in which the population is thinly spread over a large area and has little integrated public transport, and denser urban-suburban areas in the East where driving distances are shorter and alternative transport is sometimes available. Although driving to work is popularly spoken of as the "essential driving" in contrast with other "discretionary" driving, a number of studies suggest that that idea is wrong.

The point to keep in mind is that people's gasoline "needs" and "habits" or the strengths of their "demands"—the cost and pain of getting along with a uniformly modest amount or of doing so suddenly before there can be a change in vehicles, transport habits and living arrangements—will be great. Gasoline mileage alone differs by a factor of four from the "gas guzzlers" (often older, second-hand cars owned by people who cannot afford new cars) to the modern imports. There is therefor a strong tension between the principles of simplicity and equal treatment on the one hand, and discriminating or discriminatory rations based on customary consumption, commuting distance, or health and family status, on the other. It is not easy to visualize just what socio-economic classes or regions, localities and occupations, would be the conspicuous beneficiaries of a multi-category rationing formula.

Any rationing scheme, simple or complex, will have arbitrary features. A scheme that makes no allowance for mileage is arbitrary. A scheme that makes a mileage allowance on the basis of make, year, and body style, will look arbitrary.

Any but the most short-lived scheme is likely to generate a widespread system of local appeal boards. Like draft boards these may be volunteer activities. Also like draft boards, they may work with a "quota" that allows redistributing gasoline rations within an area but without enlarging the local claim on the national supply. How such ration boards would work can only be imagined, especially since wartime ration boards worked within the context of multifarious rations. And, as mentioned, there was a war on. An important consideration will be whether rationing is thought of as nearly permanent, warranting a network of appeal boards and adjudicatory procedures, or instead is conceived as short-lived and suitably left arbitrary.

Marketable and Non-Transferable Rations

We come now to the single most important philosophical issue in rationing. Should rations be marketable? Should the buying and selling of rations be not only legal but *encouraged* and *facilitated* to minimize uncertainty in the ration market, to hold down the cost and nuisance of trading in coupons, to facilitate intertemporal and interregional sales and purchases—with the daily quotations presumably shown along with the state lottery numbers on the front pages of newspapers, quoted on the 11 o'clock news, and posted at the service stations?

Before going into the pros and cons of marketable coupons, it is worthwhile noticing how such a system works in its economic effects. Assuming that the ration is effective—i.e., that the coupons distributed are within the amounts of gasoline available to the market, and that with non-transferable coupons there would be unsatisfied demand at the current price—coupons will have a positive price. People who want gas in excess of their rations will obtain coupons by paying for them. People who would rather have cash for some of their coupons than purchase gas with them will sell them. If the market is allowed and encouraged to work well, there should be only a minute margin between the price I pay for extra coupons and the price I get from selling some.

The "cost" of burning gasoline, both for the person who burns more than his normal ration and for the person who burns less, selling some of his tickets, will be *the pump price plus the value of the coupon*. That is plain for the person who buys a coupon for, say, 50¢, and turns it in to buy a gallon of gasoline for $1.50. Evidently the gallon costs him $2. The person who burns six gallons out of his ration of ten, selling four tickets at 50¢ apiece for $2, also "spends" $2 for each of the six gallons he burns. He pays $1.50 per gallon cash at the pump and delivers a coupon worth 50¢ cash. His net worth is down $2 as a result of the purchase, $1.50 at the pump and 50¢ foregone by surrendering the coupon. Indeed, if a person immediately sold his coupons upon receiving his weekly ration and then bought coupons whenever he needed gas, he could think of his ration as just $5 a week in cash, converting the ten coupons at 50¢ apiece into a $5 bill every week. He then spends $2 a gallon for whatever gas he burns, whether within or above his ration.

If the market works well and the coupons are literally pieces of paper that people carry in their wallets and deliver at the gas station, they may even come to be passed around as money, making more vivid that the "cost" of gasoline is the pump price plus the coupon value.

Notice that marketable coupons not only redistribute gasoline among drivers but redistribute it by locale and across time. There can be a net sale of coupons in Massachusetts and a net purchase in California. There can be a net sale in summer and a net purchase in winter for a family or for a locality. (The gasoline has to be free to follow the coupons; an allocation system geared to the initial distribution of coupons would ruin the coupon market, but of course an allocation system is not needed.)

The gas price could be, but need not be, controlled in a rationing scheme. That is, rationing can be coupled with price control to eliminate the ensuing problem of excess demand. It can also be used in the absence of price control to restrain demand and to keep prices from rising. Rationing can be quantitatively flexible; if the allowed demand needs to be adjusted, this is easily done with variable-quantity coupons or supplementary coupons that are validated by announcement.

There are two main arguments in favor of the full marketability of rations. One is the obvious point that if some people would rather have the money than the gasoline while others would rather pay the price and have the gasoline, just about everybody is better off being allowed to buy and sell coupons. It is sometimes countered that the well-to-do can have all the gas they want if coupons are marketable, and it is the poor who will be forced by a rationing scheme to save gas—the poor being unable to resist the temptation to convert their coupons into cash. But it is no help to the poor that, to induce them to burn their share of the gasoline when they might rather have cash, they are denied the opportunity to trade the coupons. It is precisely those who would rather have money than gasoline, because they are poor or because they have comparatively less use for gasoline than for the other things that money will buy, who are induced by the higher price to conserve gas. With non-transferable coupons, a coupon that might have been worth 50¢, together with $1.50, will buy you a gallon of gas at the pump; with marketable coupons worth 50¢ a gallon, a coupon and $1.50 will also buy a $2 gallon of milk. With marketable coupons the poor, or anybody else, can choose to have the gasoline they would have had in a non-transferable system, or to treat the coupons as financial claims that can be converted into cash.

The other argument is that marketable coupons are far more resilient to the inevitable errors and arbitrariness in the system. With non-transferable coupons, a ration that proves wholly inadequate to the special needs of an individual might be almost disastrous, unless the person could find his way around the law. With marketable coupons, the damage is limited to some percentage of the value of the extra gasoline he needs. Similarly, any beneficiary of a ration in excess of needs does not necessarily subtract from the aggregate supply; he has an incentive to feed it back into the market, legally, and to his advantage.

Once people get used to the idea that their weekly ration is a kind of "entitlement" that has a cash value, and that the "cost" of every gallon consumed is the pump price plus the coupon price, they may come to recognize that the system is not much different from a weekly cash benefit coupled with a gasoline tax. Specifically, a ten-gallon weekly ration with coupons selling at 50¢ and gas at the pump selling for $1.50, the weekly coupons are not essentially different from $5 in cash. And gasoline costs $2, whether one buys it with his own coupons or with somebody else's that he has purchased. The coupon price is not essentially different from a 50-cent tax on gasoline, everybody getting a fully refundable tax credit on ten gallons per week. Since every coupon sold is a coupon bought and vice versa, the total proceeds from selling coupons must equal the total expenditure on coupons. And the market value of all the coupons issued any week is equivalent to the cash value of each week's "entitlement." Thus the system is, except for appearance, exactly equivalent to a 50-cent gasoline tax on every gallon sold, coupled with a rebate system in which all tax proceeds are distributed precisely in accordance with what would have been a rationing scheme, i.e., to every individual who would have had ration coupons, in proportion to the coupons his ration would have allowed. While everybody may know that his $5 weekly cash benefit comes from a gasoline tax, nobody would need to pay any attention to the origin of the funds. Thus, whether one receives $5 cash or $5 worth of coupons weekly might eventually make no difference.

A Tax on Gasoline

What we have, then, with fully marketable ration coupons is a system that in its actual working is really no different from a combination of gasoline tax and rebate system. The rebate being independent of the gasoline that any individual actually purchases, the full incentive effect of the gasoline tax on the cost of consuming a gallon is unaffected by the rebate, the rebate exactly uses up the tax proceeds, and the rebate is exactly equivalent to the market price that the coupons would have yielded under a rationing scheme.

This equivalence between marketable rations and a gasoline tax coupled with a rebate system seems to be not generally recognized. But it seems likely that if the marketable system were in effect very long people would quickly perceive that that "cost" of gasoline was the sum of the pump price and the coupon value, and that everybody receives a cash allowance that exactly compensated for the "tax" on the amount that the ration would allow. People might be just as happy to receive cash in the mail every week rather than coupons, and to pay their 50¢ as a gas "tax" rather than to pay 50¢ for a "coupon."

That being so, we could probably save all the problems of printing coupons, policing the market for counterfeit coupons, and channeling the coupons through the distribution system to the point where the government monitored the outflow of distilled products against the reverse flow of coupons. Simplicity, if not public relations, would suggest doing it all with money. But maybe not until people had learned by experience that it works out just the same as money.

There is, of course, a difference between coupons whose market price can fluctuate and the gas tax that is specific in cents per gallon. In the event of an unexpected surge in demand or shortfall in supply, the gas price could rise and generate substantial windfall profits somewhere in the system. Taxes on corporate profits, or on excess profits tax, could be levied on oil companies and gasoline distributors. Alternatively, the gasoline tax at the pump could be allowed to vary with the price of gasoline. To provide retailers and wholesalers and others with an incentive to respond to the market, a small fraction of the price increase might be left untaxed, and a larger part captured by the tax. A tax that took four cents out of five on the price above some base price would leave the price free to fluctuate, provide an incentive for price adjustments at the pump, and capture the larger part of any price increase to feed back into the rebate system.

In any event, "genuine" cost increases would have to be allowed, i.e., tax-excused; but the same would be true under a rationing system with controlled prices, which would have to be adjusted for such things as changes in the price of imported crude oil.

A Summing Up

I find the case in favor of marketable coupons, if there is to be a rationing system, altogether conclusive. It permits the poor to have money if they need it more than a gasoline ration. It permits anyone, rich or poor, who badly needs additional gasoline, to get it for a price. It limits the harm inherent in rations that cannot be finely attuned, or even coarsely attuned, to the individual needs of different people. The argument that it is unfair to the poor is wholly misconceived. It is poverty that is unfair to the poor, not letting the poor convert an entitlement to gasoline into the cash with which they can buy gasoline *or* whatever else they need more than gas. The flexibility of marketable rations lets people "save" their rations for good weather or bad, for periodic or episodic needs, without having to store flammable fluids somewhere. It makes people who insist on more gasoline than the average pay for it at a price that compensates those who are induced to give it up.

The effects on law enforcement are twofold, and I am not sure which way the balance goes. Counterfeit coupons are a much greater hazard when coupons are transferable, because possession of counterfeit coupons cannot be prima facie evidence that the person who attempts to pass counterfeit coupons acquired them knowingly. At the same time, the more awkward and dangerous black market in gasoline itself, and the inducements to gasoline theft, would undoubtedly be less severe with an open market rather than a black market system.

So the first step in an argument that taxing is better than rationing is that marketable rations are vastly superior to a non-transferable coupon system. The second step then is merely the recognition that marketable rations are not much different from cash, that anyone who might have received ration coupons could receive cash instead, that the "cost" per gallon of gasoline is the same with marketable rations as with a tax-rebate system, as long as the rebate, like the rations, are received independent of the use of gasoline.

There is of course a political difference. The ration system inherently and automatically provides that "entitlement" with a money value to the people who are awarded a claim for gasoline, people with cars and driver's licenses, people who commute to work or use their cars in business, people who have large families or small, and more or less need to drive, under either a system of uniform rations or variable rations. But the coupons in principle go to people who would drive, and the money value of the coupons therefore accrues to those who would drive. With a tax-rebate system, the equivalent of the ration system can be exactly duplicated. But it need not be. There is a wider choice of who should get the rebate than there is of who should get gasoline coupons. Larger rebates for the poor would be an easy way to augment a poverty program; abolishing rebates for the wealthy would be like a "progressive" change in the income tax. Just as farmers may prefer price supports to income subsidies because they are linked to what farmers do, some people may prefer rations for fear that, having traded them in for a cash rebate under an alternative system, a congressional ways and means committee may take away the rebate.

Whether that is a virtue or a defect of the tax system depends on whose side you are on.

GASOLINE PRICES, TAXES, AND DEMAND
by William W. Hogan

The price of regular gasoline (in 1979 dollars) increased from 61 cents a gallon in 1973 to 69 cents a gallon in 1978, and then to $1 a gallon in November of 1979. The decontrol of crude oil prices and further increases in world crude oil prices could easily add another 25 to 40 cents a gallon to the price. With President Carter's proposed addition of a 10 cents a gallon tax, the price of an average gallon of regular gasoline in the United States could soon reach $1.50. This price increase of 90¢/gal since 1973 represents a substantial transfer of wealth, approximately 90 billion dollars per year, from gasoline consumers to the oil producers, both domestic and international, to the government of the United States, and to the refiners and distributors of gasoline. Documenting the exact division among the recipients is problematic, but there is little doubt that the great bulk of the wealth moved to oil producers, principally to foreign producers.

The inflationary impact of higher gasoline prices complicates the already heated debate over this redistribution of wealth. Although the nominal gasoline price increase represents only 5 percent of the total output of the economy and, therefore, should have added only 5 percent to the overall price level over the last seven years, gasoline prices are highly visible and enter directly into the calculation of the Consumer Price Index. In the vain attempt to recoup this real change in the value of gasoline, workers raise their wages and firms raise their prices in a spiral that dampens only slowly. Increases in the price of energy, therefore, have been cited as a major stimulus to the long-term increase in the rate of inflation with the attendant real losses in output. These indirect costs may be larger than the direct transfer of wealth caused by the first-round price increases themselves.

For the most part, these costs cannot be avoided. And to the extent that the higher domestic prices accommodate real changes in the world oil market, higher prices are part of the solution to our gasoline problem. It does not benefit the nation as a whole to purchase gasoline at $1.50/gal and sell it at $1.25/gal, which would be the effect of continued price controls. The consumer confronted with the full cost of gasoline will make consumption choices that reflect full cost. And a free market for

William W. Hogan is Professor of Political Economy and Director of the Energy and Environmental Policy Center at Harvard University's Kennedy School of Government. In 1975-1976, he was Deputy Assistant Administrator for Data and Analysis, Federal Energy Administration.

gasoline prices will allow producers and distributors to follow the consumer, moving gasoline in the changing mosaic of supply and demand.

The full cost of gasoline includes the indirect environmental and market externalities as well as the direct cost of production, refining, and distribution. Reasonable persons may differ on the costs of the externalities of gasoline use—for example, the costs of air and noise pollution—but we might take as a starting point the assumption that these costs were fully captured in 1973 by federal and state gasoline taxes of 10¢-12¢/gal. Given the 57 percent inflation since then, we conclude that President Carter's 10¢/gal tax increase will do little more than restore the putative balance, since all the other gasoline price increases can be attributed to changes in direct costs.

One benefit of a higher gasoline price is the stimulus it provides to reduce the demand for gasoline. The higher price will lead consumers to change their driving patterns, to moderate their driving speed, to improve the maintenance of their cars, and, gradually, to promote changes in the efficiency of the automobile fleet. These actions can bring some immediate changes in the demand for gasoline, and the changes should be more substantial over time. A recent survey[1] of the available econometric evidence suggested that the 65 percent increase in price could produce a one-year demand reduction of 5 to 10 percent, increasing to a long-run demand reduction of between 30 to 40 percent, or two to three million barrels per day.

These reductions in demand create another form of externality for gasoline that often leads to the call for further increases in the price through taxes. If the demand for gasoline falls, there will be less pressure on the world oil market, less pressure on world oil prices, and greater security for the United States. If higher gasoline prices reduce gasoline demand, so the argument goes, then these added benefits call for even higher prices through substantial increases in gasoline taxes.

Qualitatively, this argument is sound. Quantitatively, it is flawed. The calculation is usually based on the large gasoline savings forecast to accumulate as consumers adapt to the higher prices. Unfortunately, the large incremental savings are not likely to occur as the result of further price increases, at least for prices within the range of present discussion. The reason is simple. Most of the long-run savings come from consumers buying ever more efficient cars in response to the incentive of higher gasoline prices. But Congress has legislated strict standards for the corporate average fleet efficiency (CAFE) of new cars, with a schedule leading to an average efficiency of 27.5 mpg in 1985 as compared to less than 15 mpg in 1975.

The manufacturers face substantial penalties if they fail to meet these standards. Cars no better than the average 1975 model, for example, would face an effective marginal penalty of $2,300 if the fleet does not meet the standard.[2] There is little doubt that the incentive is there for the manufacturers to meet the efficiency standards. And there is little doubt that higher gasoline prices will simplify their task. But there is substantial doubt that the higher gasoline prices will be sufficient to induce the manufacturers to *exceed* the legislated standard. The most likely effect of the higher gasoline prices will be to increase the attractiveness of small cars over large, thereby causing the manufacturers to increase the price of small cars and reduce the price of large cars, at least relative to the prices that would have been required to achieve the CAFE standards at a lower gasoline price.

The econometric estimates above were based on data with no efficiency standards. They implicitly assume, therefore, that there will be no standards in the future. But common sense, and at least one detailed econometric study,[3] tells us that most of the long-run change in gasoline demand will come from a change in the efficiency of the automobile fleet. If legislation determines this fleet efficiency, and prices have no incremental effect, then we cannot attribute these higher long-run savings to the increase in gasoline prices. Recognizing that doubling the automobile efficiency halves the fuel cost of driving, we see that the improvements in efficiency will lead to some loss of the savings produced by changed driving patterns, moderation of speed, and improved maintenance. In the presence of legislated efficiency standards, a reasonable estimate is that the price-induced demand reductions are about the same in the long run as in the short run. This will hold true until the gasoline price rises enough to induce consumers, on average, to buy cars that exceed the mandatory efficiency standards.

Thus arguments for a gasoline tax—softening oil prices and improving US security—must be based on the quantitatively small short-run savings. This suggests that the best use of a tax will be as a short-run emergency measure. A large gasoline tax could be held in reserve as a weapon to use in the presence of a large supply interruption. Almost all the benefits that would flow from the tax would come in the immediate response, which will be highly valuable given the great costs of a sudden emergency.

The decontrol of crude oil prices will increase gasoline prices, but it will also stop the foolish subsidy for imported oil. The decontrol of gasoline prices may lead to no further average price increase, but it will facilitate the efficient allocation and distribution of gasoline supplies. President Carter's 10¢ gasoline tax will do little more than restore the real value of 1973 gasoline taxes to cover the cost of gasoline use externalities. A further gasoline tax should be held in reserve for an oil emergency.

The equity problems created by these gasoline price increases remain as a challenge. But there seems to be little merit to the view that these wealth distribution problems are solved best by controlling the price of gasoline and providing a triple subsidy to the wealthy family with three cars as compared to the poorer family with a single automobile. There are other avenues for income redistribution that are better for the disadvantaged and have no side effects of helping foreign oil producers.

NOTES

Data Sources: Various issues of *Monthly Energy Review, Economic Report of the President.* Figures converted with GNP inflation.

1. Pindyck, R., "The Characteristic of Energy Demand," in J. Sawhill, ed., *Energy Conservation and Public Policy,* Englewood Cliffs, N.J., Prentice-Hall, 1979.

2. Sweeney, J., in *Energy Tax Proposals Relating to Transportation,* Committee on Ways and Means of the House of Representatives, June 6, 1977, p. 25.

3. Sweeney, J., "U.S. Gasoline Demand: An Economic Analysis of the EPCA New Car Efficiency Standard," in R. Pindyck, ed., *Advances in the Economics of Energy and Resources,* Greenwich, Connecticut, 1979.

COPING WITH PETROLEUM SUPPLY INTERRUPTIONS

by Alvin L. Alm

Much of the world's petroleum supply is dependent on the political stability of a handful of countries in the Persian Gulf. The logistical system for supplying the world with petroleum is extremely vulnerable to sabotage and destruction, stretching from pipelines and refineries in the producing areas, through the narrow Strait of Hormuz to thousands of miles of open ocean. Sometime within the next few years, the Persian Gulf area will likely experience a war, revolution, natural disaster, threat of diplomatic blackmail, or accumulation of these threats that will place unacceptable economic and political strain on the political system of the Western world, unless adequate provisions are made now.

The strategic petroleum reserve, which will eventually contain 750 million to 1 billion barrels of crude oil, is designed to minimize domestic turmoil and skyrocketing spot market prices. But the strategic reserve currently contains only 92 million barrels of crude oil, about five days consumption, and will take many years to fill to target levels. In the meantime, the US must rely on other measures to reduce demand and allocate shortfalls during energy emergencies.

The best way to understand the tools a government has at its disposal to cope with supply interruptions is to take the reader through a hypothetical episode. Let us assume a specific scenario—that six million barrels per day of world oil production is terminated from the Persian Gulf. We will not say why. Because the transportation system has many protracted links, the first effects of that cut-back are not felt by end-users for two to three months after production stops.

During this early period, when there is little knowledge about the duration of the interruption, the government would urge voluntary conservation efforts. Exhorting drivers to observe the 55 mile per hour speed limit, and urging homeowners to lower thermostats are both fixtures of the first stages of a supply interruption.

When it becomes apparent that voluntary conservation efforts will have a minimal effect, stronger medicine will be served up. The next step in escalation is use of federal allocation authorities. Since petroleum products destined for homes, factories, and airplanes are considered necessary for either economic or health reasons, the government will be forced to use its

Alvin Alm is director of the Study on Environmental Quality and Industrial Fuel Decisions at the Energy and Environmental Policy Center at Harvard University's Kennedy School. He was Assistant Secretary of Energy for Policy and Evaluation from 1977 to 1979, and Assistant Administrator for Planning and Management in the Environmental Protection Agency, 1973 to 1977.

allocation authorities to stretch out supplies of gasoline. Since gasoline prices are controlled, the federal government must allocate supplies to dealers across the nation, in lieu of using the marketplace.

Lacking knowledge about potential demand under shortage conditions, the government applies some historic formula. During the summer of 1978, gasoline was allocated on the basis of the previous year's use. Since the scarcity of gasoline discouraged vacations, rural areas tended to be awash with gasoline while lines formed in urban areas. A change in the allocation formula would not have solved the problem, however, but only moved it to some other part of the distribution chain.

As the supply interruption worsens and stocks are drawn down, the gasoline lines lengthen and tempers flare. The government is expected to do something. State-imposed odd-even and minimum purchase requirements temporarily reduce lines, but by now the shortage has reached the point that efforts to lessen panic buying have only temporary salutary effects. The federal government is forced to make a very difficult decision: either eliminate price controls and allow the marketplace to allocate supplies, or impose gasoline rationing. Since lifting price controls would result in windfall profits accruing to the oil companies and retail outlets at the expense of consumers, gasoline rationing is likely to be the only acceptable political option.

At first blush, gasoline rationing does not sound that draconian except to the ardent free market enthusiast. After all, it provides, or at least seems to provide, an equitable way to distribute supplies. It is thought to have worked during World War II. In any case, it would last only as long as the emergency continues. But before accepting rationing as a good idea, we need to see how it would work.

Let us assume that the plan used is the one proposed for public comment by the Department of Energy. The coupon rationing program begins with the government's mailing out entitlement coupon books to owners of the 150 million registered vehicles (including automobiles, trucks, and buses) in the US. Let us assume that 90 percent of the entitlement books reach their destination—an optimistic assumption considering that one-third of the vehicle fleet turns over each year. That means that 10 percent of the available gasoline would not be used until owners and rationing books connect through the bureaucratic process. Once a motorist receives a rationing book, assuming some measure of luck, he or she can go to a bank or other designated place, and redeem it for rationing coupons. The banks, which can barely keep up with regular accounts, would be expected to deal with this new onslaught of work by training thousands of new, temporary employees. It is not hard to imagine gasoline lines being replaced by long lines at redemption centers. And it is far from certain where the armored cars and vaults will come from to handle this new currency.

The magnitude of the management challenge is only part of the problem. Billions of dollars of a new currency will provide enticing opportunities for counterfeiting. Exceptions and special allocations will require a new bureaucracy to deal with a myriad of special circumstances and the entreaties of special interest groups. Farmers, doctors, social workers, taxicab drivers, traveling salesmen, and many other groups will plead special circumstances requiring either class or case-by-case decisions. Since the DOE proposal will allocate rationing coupons on the basis of registered vehicles, there will be a strong incentive for motorists to buy junk cars to increase their allocation of this new currency. Finally, there is no guarantee that available gasoline supplies will catch up with demand. Since gasoline prices will be controlled, no incentives will exist to shift around supplies as demand inevitably shifts, probably away from rural areas. At worst, motorists may have rationing tickets that cannot be used because of mismatches between supply and demand.

This description of the rationing system might seem uncharitable. In fact, it greatly understates the magnitude of one of the greatest management challenges of our time. Rationing would require the creation of an entirely new currency in the period of a few months. Twenty billion coupons would be needed for the first year, compared to only 8 billion units of paper money in circulation.

But obviously, with enough time and resources, gasoline rationing could at least work at a respectable level. The only problem is that in an emergency there is no time: the chaos of gasoline rationing would probably last throughout the period of our hypothetical 6 million barrels per day cutback.

If rationing is bound to fail in meeting a large supply interruption now, why do many recall its working during World War II? Part of the explanation is the same type of nostalgia that makes the 1950s seem like an interesting period today. In fact, rationing broke down before the end of the war, as black markets cropped up and inequities became more apparent. Large disparities in gasoline developed in different parts of the country. By 1943, East Coast allocations would have allowed only 4800 miles of driving, while in other states east of the Rockies, gasoline availability was sufficient to allow 5250 to 6550 miles of driving.[1] Local rationing boards were required to make innumerable decisions on extra gasoline allocations. The examples of inequities and counterfeiting caused a school official in Springfield, Massachusetts, to exclaim that "Rationing is producing a nation of liars."[2]

But other factors were even more important. During World War II, the entire transportation infrastructure was different, with relatively compact urban areas, heavy reliance on mass transit, and only 30 million motor vehicles on the road. The great upsurge in suburbia and personal transportation is a post-World War II phenomenon. Gasoline rationing was phased in over a number of years during World War II, which allowed administrative problems to be worked out. Finally, because the war effort was widely supported and most families had relatives whose lives were at stake, or perceived to be at stake, there was a greater willingness to make sacrifices. Clearly, the World War II experience is not applicable today.

Even if gasoline rationing is an administrative monstrosity, are there any realistic alternatives? Is it possible to allow gasoline price increases to allocate supplies during a serious supply interruption, creating huge (although temporary) windfall profits to oil companies and retail outlets? Before answering these questions, it is useful to discuss how rationing actually provides equity.

The DOE gasoline rationing plan calls for creation of a white market system that would allow rationing coupons to be bought and sold. If a motorist had sufficient money and valued driving heavily, he or she could buy more tickets at a white market center. Those who valued other goods or services more highly, or did not have need for all the coupons issued, could sell them at the center. (The white market approach is particularly equitable for the poor, who could trade gasoline coupons for necessities.) The value of tickets, along with the controlled price of gasoline, would represent the market value of gasoline. For example, if tickets were worth $1.50 and the controlled price was $1.50, the market value of gasoline would be three dollars. Under rationing, consumers would receive the windfalls for all tickets that were sold.

If gasoline prices were decontrolled, however, oil companies would receive windfalls from sale of gasoline at the market clearing price.[3] Rationing has the effect of preventing windfall profits to producers and creating a source of revenues for consumers. Hence, we face a dilemma. While rationing has positive equity benefits, it would pose almost insuperable administrative problems.

There are, however, ways to achieve the same equity benefits and still use the superior qualities of the marketplace to allocate supplies. Suppose that instead of sending motorists rationing coupons worth a dollar, the federal government sent them cash, collected from a temporary windfall profits tax imposed during an emergency. Instead of redeeming coupons, buying or selling them, and putting up with a host of other administrative complexities, motorists could make choices in the marketplace with money instead of coupons. The price of gasoline under such a system would now be much higher, but incomes would also be proportionately higher.

Such a system might work as follows:

1. Crude oil prices would be decontrolled during the course of a supply interruption, allowing prices to rise naturally to market levels, before, during, and after the interruption. This will avoid the need for government management of the supply system.

2. An emergency windfall tax would be imposed on domestic oil producers, refiners, and distributors. The windfall profits tax would collect up to 90 percent of any final price increase not associated with average crude oil costs. The tax would be levied on increases over the base price for producers, and over the base mark-ups for refiners, wholesalers, and retailers of gasoline. The size of the tax, therefore would fluctuate according to the emergency market conditions, automatically disappearing if the price dropped to the base price. By recouping only 90 percent of the windfall, an adequate incentive would be provided for efficient allocation of the limited supplies.

3. The windfall tax would be rebated directly to the public. At worst, the proceeds of the tax could be rebated to the registered owners of automobiles, and be as fair as the proposed gasoline rationing scheme. Or, rebates would be given to all households, a distribution mechanism that passed the House of Representatives to allocate revenue from President Carter's proposed Crude Oil Equalization Tax. Since the poor spend less for energy than the affluent, a per household rebate would be substantially more progressive than any system conferring economic benefits only on owners of vehicles. To prevent inequities and "fiscal drag," tax withholding rates could be automatically adjusted during the course of a supply interruption.

But would not a new emergency windfall profits tax create a

whole host of new complexities? How would a base price be calculated? How would higher costs of crude oil be passed through? How can you prevent inequities to independent refiners and retailers? The list could go on and on.

Although administrative problems would crop up with a tax-rebate scheme, there are important distinctions between these problems and those that would be faced by gasoline rationing. The latter would create a new administrative superstructure and bureaucracy, while the former would rely on the well-administered Internal Revenue Service. The latter would directly affect millions of Americans, while the former would be confined to the oil industry. The latter would require "breaking new ground" at every step, including creation of a duplicate currency, while the former would require adjustments to the tax system with definitions and data to be derived from the current oil price control program.

Only a perpetual optimist can view the next decade without foreseeing one or more serious supply interruptions. Considering this high probability, the predictable administrative problems that would ensue from rationing, and the fact that alternatives are available to allocate supplies with the same equity benefits, it is time to give the highest priority to developing market alternatives to rationing. But, we seem immobilized, realizing that rationing will likely not work but unwilling to consider options. If we wait until a crisis occurs, we may find ourselves slipping inexorably toward a rationing program that can only result in chaos, and a strengthening of the perception that government is no longer capable of competent and effective action.

1. James A. Maxwell, "Gasoline Rationing in the United States," *Quarterly Journal of Economics,* 60 (1946), 561; 61 (1946), 125.

2. *New York Times,* Editorial, February 10, 1980.

3. The windfalls to producers and consumers would probably be temporary. As shortages occurred, OPEC and other producing countries would raise crude oil prices. A combination of higher prices and easing of shortages would, over time, bring supply and demand in balance. The ability of controls to keep prices down is ephemeral, as can be witnessed by the current high gasoline prices still under federal price controls.

PUBLIC OPINION AND THE ENERGY CRISIS

by William Schneider

In his dramatic speech after descending from his Camp David redoubt last summer, President Carter pounded the table and proclaimed, "The energy crisis is real. It is worldwide. It is a clear and present danger to our nation. These are facts."

The President probably knew that he was speaking to an audience of nonbelievers. CBS News and the *New York Times* have been asking a national sample of Americans periodically since the summer of 1977 whether "the shortage of oil we hear about is real" or "are we just being told there are shortages so oil companies can charge higher prices?" In 1977 and 1978, about half of the public said that "we are just being told there are shortages," while about 40 percent said that the shortages are "real." Strikingly, as gasoline lines grew longer, the belief that the energy crisis is contrived became more prevalent. In early July 1979, just before the President's speech, the margin of disbelief was over two to one (26 percent said that the shortages are "real" and 66 percent felt they were being handed a line). Just after the President's speech, the view that the crisis is "real" increased slightly, to 35 percent, but a majority of the public, 53 percent, persisted in the belief that no real shortage exists. The Roper poll shows the same result: as gasoline lines grew longer and prices increased, more and more Americans said that "there never was any real oil shortage—it was contrived for economic and political reasons."

At the same time, more people have been saying that the energy crisis is a "serious" problem and naming it as one of the most important issues facing the country. How can people believe that the problem is "serious" but not "real"?

From the public's point of view, events have tended to confirm the impression that shortages are being deliberately manipulated. Consider what happened in the 1973-1974 crisis and again last year. First there were reported shortages resulting in long lines at service stations. Then the price of gasoline increased sharply and—almost instantaneously—the shortages vanished and gasoline was plentiful again. "There's plenty of oil and gas," the public said. "They're just waiting to get the price they want for it."

"They" of course are the oil companies. Polls asking people

William Schneider, a Visiting Fellow at the Hoover Institution at Stanford University, is spending 1980 as an International Affairs Fellow of the Council on Foreign Relations. A specialist in public opinion and voting behavior, he holds a Ph.D. in political science from Harvard University, where he previously taught. He is co-author with S.M. Lipset of *How Americans View Their Institutions* (Macmillan, 1981).

whom they blame for the energy crisis have consistently shown the oil companies at the top of the list, usually by a wide margin. The Arab countries and the US government also receive a share of the blame, but not nearly so much as the oil companies. In June 1979, according to the Roper poll, 72 percent blamed the oil companies, 51 percent blamed the Arabs, 36 percent blamed the Administration, and 34 percent blamed Congress.

Most Americans believe that we have to import some oil from other countries to meet our present energy needs, but a stubborn—and growing—minority feels that we produce enough oil in this country to meet our needs. According to the Gallup poll, the view that we are self-sufficient was held by 33 percent in 1977, 27 percent in 1978, 38 percent in 1979, and 41 percent in February 1980. One possible explanation is the public's confidence that American knowhow will provide alternative energy sources within a decade. The President has encouraged this belief by calling for massive investment in alternative energy sources. Not surprisingly, the public tends to favor steps to accelerate the development of new energy sources— including nuclear energy, by a small margin—and to oppose most measures to conserve energy (penalty taxes, rationing, higher energy prices).

The accompanying figure indicates what energy resources people feel we can rely on for the future. The public sees oil as our principal energy source "this year" but believes it will decline sharply in the near future and then fade into insignificance. The same trend is projected for natural gas. Coal is perceived as increasing in importance in the immediate future (2 to 5 years) but declining thereafter. Nuclear and solar power are seen as increasing in importance and becoming dominant in the medium-range and distant future, with solar power eventually moving into first place. These expectations are fairly reasonable, at least in relative terms, although the time-frame is notably foreshortened (the public expects solar and nuclear energy to be the principal sources of electrical energy within 6 to 10 years).

Americans are not wholly unrealistic about the limited availability of energy resources or about their own wasteful habits (61 percent say that most Americans are "highly wasteful" in their use of energy). But they do not feel that these "facts" adequately explain the energy crisis. The energy crisis is perceived, like so many other ills these days, as an *abuse of power*. Events such as the reports of oil company profits serve more nearly to confirm than to contradict this belief. What the oil companies, OPEC, and the federal government have in common is that they are seen to be powerful, monopolistic, and irrespon-

Figure 1
Current and Future Sources of Energy:
The Public's View, 1979

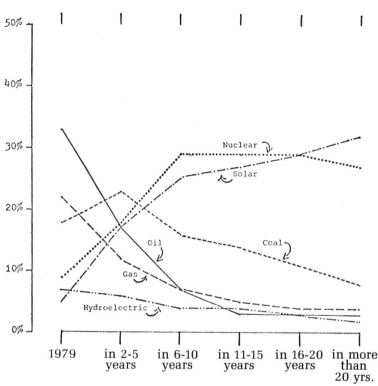

Source: ABC News/Harris Survey, April 6-9, 1979

sible. They are capable of abusing the public interest, and the public clearly believes they do so.

When it comes to policies for dealing with the energy crisis, the poll data reveal a tremendous sensitivity to the issue of price. The majority rejects any solution that has the effect of raising the cost of fuel by a significant amount.

Consider the issue of gasoline rationing. The polls indicate that rationing is not popular, unless it is described specifically as "standby authority" to ration gasoline in an emergency. When the Roper poll offered a proposal to "ration natural gas, gasoline, and heating oil to guarantee fair but reduced supplies to all," it was opposed, 59 to 32 percent.

Basically, there are three ways to ration gasoline: by physical allocation, by price, or by inconvenience. Cambridge Survey Research offered respondents a choice among all three in a poll taken in February 1979. The first choice, preferred by 45 percent, was "a system of coupon rationing where all automobile drivers would be permitted to buy a particular number of gallons of gasoline every week using the ration coupons." The second most popular option, preferred by 22 percent, was "allowing gasoline prices to increase so that vehicle usage would be discouraged and gasoline consumption would go down." The least favored alternative was "a system of allocation where each part of the country would be permitted only so much gasoline, and rationing would essentially take place as it did during the 1973-74 oil embargo, since people would have to wait in lines and stations would close when they ran out of gasoline." Only 16 percent expressed a desire to repeat that experience. But, of course, that experience was repeated.

Thus rationing is favored as an alternative, but only as an alternative, to the less desirable options of price increases and shortages.

A $2 A GALLON POLITICAL OPPORTUNITY

by Robert H. Williams

The President, in his State-of-the-Union address, indicated that military force might be used to protect vital US interests in the Persian Gulf. A more effective response to the threat to US security posed by recent events in the Middle East would be for the President to set the nation on a course which would lead to a significant reduction, and even phasing out, of US oil imports from insecure foreign sources.

A proposal along these lines, involving a stiff gasoline tax along with a prescription for returning the tax revenues to taxpayers, is set forth in this paper.[1] This scheme would be immediately effective in curbing gasoline demand. It would be progressive, allow for a major reduction in existing corporate taxes, and involve relatively minor administrative costs.

Refunding the Revenues

The purpose of the added gasoline tax is to curb the demand for gasoline—not generate increased revenues. It is important to keep funds in the hands of consumers so that individuals can buy more fuel-efficient autos, so that firms can create van pooling programs for their employees, and so that, in general, fuel saving investments can be made more readily.

Thus, the added gasoline tax revenues should be returned to consumers. Because many people suspect that a new gasoline tax would be used to generate increased revenues, it is important politically to pass the legislation specifying how the revenues would be refunded *before* passing the gasoline tax legislation.

The refund scheme proposed here involves (1) rebating to all adults (via the Internal Revenue Service) the new gasoline tax arising from motor vehicles in personal use and (2) reducing either corporate income taxes or employer contributions to Social Security with the new gasoline tax revenues that arise from motor vehicles used by businesses.

Setting the Level of the Tax

It is proposed that the gasoline tax be raised from $0.12 to $2.00 a gallon.* There are several reasons for such a large increase.

---

*The tax should be established by law in constant dollars—i.e., the tax should be indexed to inflation. Otherwise inflation will kill the tax over time. The gasoline tax in the US was reduced by 60 percent in constant dollars between 1959 and 1980, even though the tax was constant in current dollars.

Robert H. Williams is Senior Research Physicist at the Center for Energy and Environmental Studies. He is co-author with Marc Ross of *Our Energy: Regaining Control* (McGraw Hill, 1980). Dr. Williams is also on the steering committee of the American Council for an Energy-Efficient Economy.

For one, the price paid by the consumer for gasoline should reflect both the direct cost of gasoline and the added social cost arising from increased dependence on foreign oil. While a tax increase of $1.88 a gallon (about $80 a barrel) is more than most investigators have estimated as the social cost of increased oil imports, these estimates do not adequately take into account the cost of security from oil supply disruption.[2] Until recently this cost could be estimated rather simply as the cost of building the Strategic Petroleum Reserve, *assuming that extra oil supplies would be available for such a stockpile.* Today this cost is much more difficult to calculate and must be far higher than previous estimates.[3]

It is also clear that the tax must be very high to achieve significant near-term gasoline savings. For the tax scheme proposed here, gasoline demand might be reduced about 10 percent in the first year, and more in successive years.[4]

By raising the tax to $2, the US would also demonstrate to its allies the seriousness of its commitment to dealing with the world oil crisis. A $2 tax would just bring the US into the lead in this effort, since some Western European nations already have gasoline taxes nearly this large. (In January 1980 the tax on regular gasoline was $1.62 a gallon in France and $1.83 a gallon in Italy.)

Finally, a tax of the magnitude proposed would not be burdensome in the long run if a transition were made to fuel-efficient autos. *The owner of a 40-45 mpg car would pay no more per mile for gasoline taxed at $2.00 a gallon than would the owner of the average car on the road today pay for gasoline taxed at the present rate.* A review of automotive technological opportunities indicates that the average fuel economy of new cars could be raised to the 40-45 mpg level by the 1990s.[5]

Rebating the Tax to Adults

The extra gasoline tax revenues arising from motor vehicles in personal use would amount to about $120 billion in the first year of the tax. If these revenues were rebated equally to all adults (those persons 16 years of age and older), the rebate would amount to about $730 per adult in the first year.[6]

To see how this scheme would affect different groups using automobiles and light trucks for personal use, estimates of what various households would pay for gasoline are needed. In this connection it is useful to introduce the concept of the "effective price" of gasoline. The effective price is the total net expenditure for gasoline (the actual expenditures minus the rebate) divided by total gasoline consumption.[7]

Figure 1

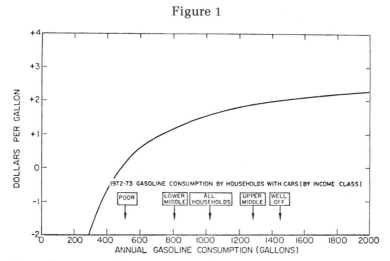

The effective gasoline price is calculated according to the prescription in Note 7. Consumption estimates by income level are from Note 8.

Figure 1 shows the effective gasoline price in the first year for different levels of gasoline consumption by a household with two adults. It is evident that the effective price varies markedly with the level of consumption. While big gasoline consumers could end up paying twice today's gasoline price, for those who conserve, the effective price could be substantially below today's price (even zero or negative!). Note that if annual consumption levels for different income groups were the same as the 1972-73 levels,[8] the average household would be paying an effective price of about $1.55 a gallon, the well-off $2.00 a gallon, but the poor only $0.10 a gallon!

The assumption that gasoline consumption levels would remain at the 1972-73 levels is of course unrealistic. People would adjust their consumption habits in response to the higher marginal gasoline price, which would be $3.00 a gallon for all households. Moreover, many households already have cars with greater fuel economy than those in typical use in 1972-73. It is useful therefore to note the conditions under which consumers could beat the tax, i.e., pay an effective price of no more than $1.10 a gallon.

As shown in Figure 1, the average household could beat the tax by reducing annual consumption by about 25 percent to 770 gallons a year. Such a reduction could be achieved either by driving less or by using a more fuel-efficient car. For the typical household, driving about 14,000 miles per year, the tax could be neutralized by a 19 mpg fuel economy (see Figure 2).

But what about the poor, many of whom must drive the discarded behemoths of the more affluent? The program proposed here would actually benefit the poor. As shown in Table A, nearly half of poor households in 1972-73 had no cars, and those that did drove only about half as much as the average household. Thus a car-less two-adult household would get a net income supplement of nearly $1500 in the first year, while a car-owning poor household driving 8000 miles per year could beat the gas tax in the first year with a fuel economy of 10 mpg or more (see Figure 2). It is unclear precisely what the net effect on gasoline consumption by the poor would be with the gasoline tax/rebate scheme proposed here. However, a rough calculation indicates that since the rebate would lead to such a large fractional increase in income, gasoline consumption by the poor may even increase slightly when this scheme is implemented![4]

Thus a gasoline tax rebated to all adults would provide substantial benefits to most of the poor, while giving all consumers an immediate powerful incentive to conserve.

It is to be expected that the rebates would decline over time as gasoline demand diminishes. However, this decline would be very gradual, giving consumers ample time to adjust their consuming habits and to purchase more fuel-efficient cars. The consumer who responds to the $3 gasoline price by buying a 37

Figure 2

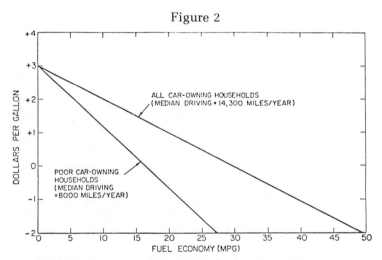

EFFECTIVE GASOLINE PRICE FOR TWO ADULT CAR-OWNING HOUSEHOLDS

mpg car would be able to beat the tax even if the rebate were eventually reduced in half.[10] Moreover, his effective annual gasoline bill with the 37 mpg car would be only 40 percent as much as it would be at today's gasoline price for a 14 mpg behemoth.[11]

Shifting Corporate Taxes

The net extra gasoline tax revenues from business use of motor vehicles would amount to over $25 billion.[12] While corporations would account for less than 20 percent of the total revenues from the gasoline tax, the revenue from corporations would be sufficient to allow for an across-the-board reduction* in corporate income taxes or employer contributions to Social Security of nearly 40 percent.[13]

Implementing the Tax Program

Rebating the gasoline tax revenues to adults could be achieved rather simply by adding a line to the individual income tax form, where the taxpayer would indicate the number of adults in the household. While not all people file income tax forms, this program would provide everyone with the incentive to do so, because the rebate scheme would be in essence a negative income tax for those who do not pay taxes.

Because the tax revenues would be so large (about $150 billion in the first year, equivalent to one-third of federal tax receipts from all sources in 1979) it is important to recycle the gasoline tax revenues rapidly. This might be accomplished by reducing withholding taxes.

Of course, some groups would have to be given special attention. First, it may be desirable not to distribute rebates equally among all adults—at least initially. Rather, the magnitude of the rebate might be varied somewhat with the region of the country, to take into account differing degrees of dependence on the automobile.

Second, it may be necessary to "prebate" the tax revenues to low income households for which the full rebate could not be effected through reduced withholding. Special attention would also have to be given to the poor who drive a lot. While the median amount of driving by poor households with cars is 8000 miles per year, 20 percent of poor households with cars (or 10 percent of all poor households) drive 15,000 miles per year or

---

*For example, the tax rate could be reduced.

Table A.
Cars, Drivers, Residential Location,
and Car Mileage by Income,
1972-1973

Cars, drivers, location, and mileage	Poor	Lower middle	Upper middle	Well off
	Percent			
All households	100	100	100	100
Cars				
No car	47	16	4	1
1	37	52	35	21
2	14	25	51	58
3 or more	2	7	10	21
Drivers				
None	34	12	2	1
1	43	39	13	7
2 or more	23	50	85	92
Drivers all households w/cars				
None	2	1	a	1
1	57	41	11	7
2 or more	41	58	89	92
Residential location				
Inside metro area	56	68	71	82
Central city	39	39	24	24
Ring	17	29	47	58
Outside metro area	44	32	29	18
Miles driven in past year[b]				
Less than 10,000	64	39	15	12
10,000-14,999	17	27	18	15
15,000 or over	20	35	67	72
	Median miles			
Miles driven in past year	8,000	12,000	18,000	20,000

[a]Less than 0.5 percent.
[b]For all cars owned 12 months or more and for which mileage was reported.

Source: See D.K. Newman and D. Day, The American Energy Consumer.

more (see Table A). But, since this problem arises for less than 2 percent of all households, it could be handled by an enhanced rebate granted to qualifying petitioners.

Similarly, special attention must be given to certain businesses. Businesses that are heavily dependent on motor vehicles should be protected, perhaps by allowing them to deduct from corporate income taxes the actual gasoline taxes paid on some fraction of their gasoline consumption. As with the personal rebates, however, such special cases will account for only a small fraction of the total number of motor vehicles. For example, there are only 200,000 taxis in the US.[14]

Finally, the tax should be applied to diesel cars. Even though such cars account for a negligible fraction of total automotive fuel use, a tax on gasoline alone would create an artificially strong demand for diesel cars. Taxing diesel fuel for autos requires that special attention be given to diesel fuel used for trucks. To prevent fraud it may be necessary to tax all diesel fuel, but also simultaneously protect truckers, perhaps in the same way gasoline-intensive businesses would be protected.

While the administrative burden associated with this program would not be negligible, it would largely involve dealing with a relatively limited set of special cases. In any case, far fewer special cases would require administrative review than with a rationing system, where the number of coupons is absolutely limited. And the tax proposal would require none of the cumbersome administrative bureaucracy required for the distribution of coupons with mandatory gasoline rationing.

The Politics of a Gasoline Tax

The fear of adverse political reaction to a gasoline tax has blinded our nation's leaders to the potential political benefits of a gasoline conservation program involving a stiff gasoline tax that is refunded.[15] The program outlined here could generate immediate and substantial gasoline savings which could lead to a reduction of our dependence on Middle Eastern and North African oil by as much as two-thirds over the next decade.[16] Moreover, typical consumers could more than offset the impact of the gasoline tax by purchasing more fuel-efficient cars. The program would be beneficial for typical poor people, and the impact of the tax on businesses could be offset by a major reduction in corporate income taxes or employer contributions to Social Security.

It may well be true that *the key to the political success of a gasoline tax proposal is that the tax be large.* If the proposed tax is modest the private gains to various beneficiaries would not be enough to provoke tough lobbying. But as this paper has shown, a stiff tax would make possible major private as well as social benefits.

One should also consider the cost of not pursuing the tax. Back in early 1977, when gasoline sold for less than $0.60 a gallon, the Carter Administration's proposal for a $0.05 a gallon standby gasoline tax was roundly defeated. Yet in less than three years the price of gasoline has risen to over $1.00 a gallon. And recently, as Shell Oil Company announced its second nickel a gallon wholesale gasoline price increase in as many weeks, Shell president John F. Bookout said to reporters "it's not all that unlikely" that United States gasoline prices will climb to the $2-a-gallon range in "late 1980 or 1981."[17] A major benefit of a true gasoline tax is that it would put a lid on the "taxes" that are being levied on us by OPEC—taxes that cannot be rebated.

1. The gasoline tax proposal set forth here is an example of a general strategy to promote energy conservation through an energy tax shift. For a general discussion of the role of energy taxes in promoting energy conservation see M.H. Ross and R.H. Williams, *Our Energy–Regaining Control,* to be published by McGraw-Hill in 1980. For the detailed calculations relating to the specific gasoline tax proposal set forth here, see Robert H. Williams, "A $2 a Gallon Political Opportunity," Center for Energy and Environmental Studies Report No. 102, Princeton University, April 14, 1980.

2. The following are three estimates of the social cost of increased oil imports, as summarized in Archie L. Wood, "The Social Cost of Imported Oil," Report prepared by TRW for Oak Ridge National Laboratory, November 28, 1979:

Various Estimates of the Premium Above Direct Costs for Incremental
Changes in US Oil Imports
($ per barrel)
Alternative Estimates

Components of per barrel costs	NORDHAUS[a]	LEMON[b]	STOBAUGH and YERGIN[c]
Change in direct oil prices	$3.00-$28.00	$12.50	$17.00
Macroeconomic effects	$10.00-$18.00	$22.42	$5.00-$55.00
Security from Supply Disruption	N.I.[d]	$.400	N.I.[d]
TOTAL	$10.00-$46.00	$38.92	$22.00-$72.00

a) Nordhaus, William D. "The Energy Crisis and Macroeconomic Policy," Cowles Foundation Discussion Paper #534, July 30, 1979 (unpublished).
b) Lemon, J.R., "The Direct and External Benefits of Reducing Oil Imports," *Energy Topics,* Supplement to *IGT Highlights,* October 1, 1979.
c) Stobaugh, R. and D. Yergin, eds., *Energy Future,* Random House, New York, 1979.
d) Not included in the estimate.

While these estimates of the added social cost of increased oil imports do not adequately take into account the cost of security from supply disruption, it is noteworthy that they are nevertheless consistent with the added gasoline tax proposed here for the situation where all the added social cost of increased imports is reflected in the price of gasoline. The proposed increase in the gasoline tax of $1.88 a gallon ($15 per million Btu) corresponds to a tax on crude oil of $6.40 per million Btu or $37 a barrel (if 43 percent of the energy content of the crude oil ends up as gasoline—the percentage for US refineries in the first 11 months of 1979, according to *Monthly Energy Review,* January 1980). This crude oil tax is comparable to the indirect social cost of increased oil imports as estimated by Lemon and is within the range of estimates of this indirect social cost provided by Nordhaus and by Stobaugh and Yergin. (In a similar manner the Administration has mandated that President Carter's oil import fee of $4.62 a barrel, imposed March 14, 1980, can be passed on to consumers only through an increase in the price of gasoline. See Richard D. Lyons, "Import Fuels Intended to Cut Foreign Oil Use," *The New York Times,* March 15, 1980.)

3. In early March 1980, Saudi Arabia's Petroleum Minister, Sheik Ahmed Zaki Yamani, warned that if the United States started to purchase oil for its strategic reserves, the move would push up prices and lead to a Saudi decision to cut back its exports. At the same time Energy Secretary Charles Duncan announced that the US would delay adding oil to its petroleum reserves for the time being. See Youssef M. Ibrahim, "Yamani Predicts Oil Price Relief But Warns U.S. on Fuel Reserve," *The New York times,* March 6, 1980.

4. Here it is assumed that the new tax revenues arising from personal use of gasoline are rebated equally among adults (those 16 years of age and older). Consumers would respond to the tax by cutting back on gasoline use but would respond to the rebate by increasing consumption, because the rebate would increase their incomes. The gasoline consumption for different income groups is assumed to be a function of the number of households, the income per household, and the price of gasoline. It is assumed that the short run price elasticity of demand for gasoline is −0.2 and that in the first year the number of households increases 2.4 percent. Income elasticities are estimated from data for 1972-73 showing gasoline consumption as a function of income. The result is that gasoline consumption overall is reduced 10 percent in the first year. However, the effect on consumption per household varies substantially with the income level:

DATA BASE FOR 1972-1973 (See Note 8).

Income Group	Percent of Households	Estimated Average Income ($)	Income Elasticity	Gasoline Consumption* (gallons/year)
Poor	18	3,000	0.83	272
Lower Middle	42	9,000	1.15	680
Upper Middle	19	15,000	0.32	1,224
Well Off	20	25,000		1,440
All Households	100			848

Consumption per Household after the Tax**

Consumption per Household before the Tax

Poor	1.014
Lower Middle	0.91
Upper Middle	0.83
Well Off	0.83
All Households	0.87

*For all households, with and without cars.
**Ratio derived by dividing Consumption per Household after Tax by Consumption per Household before Tax.

5. See the paper by Frank von Hippel in this volume.
6. Gasoline consumption for personal use of automobiles, light trucks, and motorcycles in 1977 amounted to about 67 percent of total gasoline consumption. If it is assumed that this same percentage applies to gasoline consumption in 1979 and that gasoline consumption would be reduced 10 percent in the first year after the tax is imposed (see Note 4), then the extra gasoline tax revenues from personal use of motor vehicles in the first year would be $122 billion. The rebate from these revenues would be $730 per adult since in 1980 there are 167 million adults (persons age 16 and over) in the US.
7. For a household with n adults consuming C gallons of gasoline per year the effective price P in the first year would be

$$P = 3.00 - \frac{730n}{C} \text{ dollars per gallon.}$$

It is also useful to express the effective price in terms of the fuel economy F (in miles/gallon) and the vehicle miles driven per year V:

$$P = 3.00 - \frac{73 \text{ on } F}{V} \text{ dollars per gallon}$$

8. Data on gasoline consumption by income group for 1972-3 are obtained from D.K. Newman and D. Day, *The American Energy Consumer*, a report to the Energy Policy Project of the Ford Foundation, Ballinger, Cambridge, 1975.

9. In 1976 the median number of miles driven per car-owning household was 14,300 (*Transportation Energy Conservation Data Book*, Table 1.61, p. 1-105).

10. For a two-adult household driving 14,300 miles per year when the annual rebate is $365 per adult.

11. For the conditions in Note 10 the effective annual gasoline bill would be $430. For the same amount of driving in a 14 mpg car the annual gasoline bill would be $1120 for a gasoline price of $1.10 a gallon.

12. Gasoline consumption for business use of automobiles and trucks in 1977 amounted to about 27 percent of total gasoline consumption. Assuming that in 1979 as in 1977, 27 percent of gasoline was consumed by business, that gasoline demand is reduced 10 percent in the first year after the tax is imposed, and that the corporate income tax rate is 46 percent, then net new gasoline tax revenues from businesses would be about $27 billion.

13. Federal corporate income tax receipts for 1979 are estimated to have been $70.3 billion. This is comparable to the employer contributions to Social Security. The sum of employee and employer contributions in 1979 is estimated to have been $119.7 billion (see *Statistical Abstract of the United States*, 1979, p. 258).

14. In 1977 there were 202,000 taxis in the US (*Transportation Energy Conservation Data Book*, Table 1.36, p. 1-69), each driven an average of 51,000 miles per year (op. cit., Table 1.37, p. 1-70). This represents one percent of total automobile miles driven or 0.75 percent of total gasoline consumption (see Table B).

15. A $0.50 a gallon gasoline tax has been advanced, however, by Presidential candidate John Anderson. See John B. Anderson, "For a Tax of 50 Cents on Gas," Op Ed Column in *The New York Times*, August 28, 1979.

16. It is difficult to estimate what future gasoline consumption would be with a $2.00 a gallon gasoline tax, but the following estimate for 1990:

Annual Gasoline Consumption (billion gallons)

	1977	1990
Automobiles	79.9	42.6
Light Trucks for Personal Use	10.9	11.1
Other Light Trucks	9.3	10.0
Miscellaneous	9.9	9.9
	110.0	73.6

is an "educated guess" based on the data in Table B, and the following additional assumptions:

- The average automotive fuel economy increases 70 percent (from 13.9 to 24 mpg), 1977-1990. (This would require that the average fuel economy of new cars increase steadily to 40 mpg or so by the early 1990s).
- The average light truck fuel economy increases 40 percent, 1977-1990.
- Annual use of autos and personal light trucks is reduced 25 percent, 1977-1990.
- Gasoline for uses other than autos and light trucks remains constant, 1977-1990.

Thus gasoline savings relative to the 1979 consumption level of 108 billion gallons would be 34.4 billion gallons/year or 2.24 million barrels/day. For comparison, US oil imports from Middle Eastern and North African sources totalled 3.3 million barrels/day in the first 10 months of 1979 (see *Monthly Energy Review*, January, 1980).

17. "Shell Oil Increases Gas 5¢ a Gallon," *The New York Times*, January 18, 1980.

Table B.
Auto and Single Unit Truck Projections
(millions)

	1976	1977	1990
Autos	97.8[a]	99.9[a]	121.1[b]
Single Unit Trucks	26.5[c]		
Light Trucks for Personal Use	11.0[e]	11.9[e]	22.6[d]
Other Light Trucks	9.4[e]	9.7[e]	14.6[d]
Heavier Trucks	6.1		

a) *Transportation Energy Conservation Data Book*, Edition 3, February 1979, Table 1.8, p. 1-27.

b) R. Knorr and M. Millar, "Projections of Automobile, Light Truck, and Bus Stocks and Sales, to the Year 2000," Argonne National Laboratory Report ANL/CNSV-TM-22, November 1979, Table 2.11, p. 17.

c) *Transportation Energy Conservation Data Book*, Table 1.13, p. 1-34.

d) "Projections of Automobile, Light Truck, and Bus Stocks and Sales, to the Year 2000," Table 3.7, p. 28.

e) Based on interpolation between 1975 and 1985 estimates given in Table 3.7, p. 28 of reference in note (d).

BOOKS WRITTEN UNDER CENTER AUSPICES

The Soviet Bloc, Zbigniew K. Brzezinski (sponsored jointly with the Russian Research Center), 1960. Harvard University Press. Revised edition, 1967.

The Necessity for Choice, by Henry A. Kissinger, 1961. Harper & Bros.

Rift and Revolt in Hungary, by Ferenc A. Váli, 1961. Harvard University Press.

Strategy and Arms Control, by Thomas C. Schelling and Morton H. Halperin, 1961. Twentieth Century Fund.

United States Manufacturing Investment in Brazil, by Lincoln Gordon and Engelbert L. Grommers, 1962. Harvard Business School.

The Economy of Cyprus, by A.J. Meyer, with Simos Vassiliou (sponsored jointly with the Center for Middle Eastern Studies), 1962. Harvard University Press.

Entrepreneurs of Lebanon, by Yusif A. Sayigh (sponsored jointly with the Center for Middle Eastern Studies), 1962. Harvard University Press.

Communist China 1955-1959: Policy Documents with Analysis, with a foreword by Robert R. Bowie and John K. Fairbank (sponsored jointly with the East Asian Research Center), 1962. Harvard University Press.

Somali Nationalism, by Saadia Touval, 1963. Harvard University Press.

The Dilemma of Mexico's Development, by Raymond Vernon, 1963. Harvard University Press.

Limited War in the Nuclear Age, by Morton H. Halperin, 1963. John Wiley & Sons.

In Search of France, by Stanley Hoffmann et al., 1963. Harvard University Press.

The Arms Debate, by Robert A. Levine, 1963. Harvard University Press.

Africans on the Land, by Montague Yudelman, 1964. Harvard University Press.

Counterinsurgency Warfare, by David Galula, 1964. Frederick A. Praeger, Inc.

People and Policy in the Middle East, by Max Weston Thornburg, 1964. W.W. Norton & Co.

Shaping the Future, by Robert R. Bowie, 1964. Columbia University Press.

Foreign Aid and Foreign Policy, by Edward S. Mason (sponsored jointly with the Council on Foreign Relations), 1964. Harper & Row.

How Nations Negotiate, by Fred Charles Iklé, 1964. Harper & Row.

Public Policy and Private Enterprise in Mexico, edited by Raymond Vernon, 1964. Harvard University Press.

China and the Bomb, by Morton H. Halperin (sponsored jointly with the East Asian Research Center), 1965. Frederick A. Praeger, Inc.

Democracy in Germany, by Fritz Erler (Jodidi Lectures), 1965. Harvard University Press.

The Troubled Partnership, by Henry A. Kissinger (sponsored jointly with the Council on Foreign Relations), 1965. McGraw-Hill Book Co.

The Rise of Nationalism in Central Africa, by Robert I. Rotberg, 1965. Harvard University Press.

Pan-Africanism and East African Integration, by Joseph S. Nye, Jr., 1965. Harvard University Press.

Communist China and Arms Control, by Morton H. Halperin and Dwight H. Perkins (sponsored jointly with the East Asian Research Center), 1965. Frederick A. Praeger, Inc.

Problems of National Strategy, ed. Henry Kissinger, 1965. Frederick A. Praeger, Inc.

Deterrence before Hiroshima: The Airpower Background of Modern Strategy, by George H. Quester, 1966, John Wiley & Sons.

Containing the Arms Race, by Jeremy J. Stone, 1966. M.I.T. Press.

Germany and the Atlantic Alliance: The Interaction of Strategy and Politics, by James L. Richardson, 1966. Harvard University Press.

Arms and Influence, by Thomas C. Schelling, 1966. Yale University Press.

Political Change in a West African State, by Martin Kilson, 1966. Harvard University Press.

Planning Without Facts: Lessons in Resource Allocation from Nigeria's Development, by Wolfgang F. Stolper, 1966. Harvard University Press.

Export Instability and Economic Development, by Alasdair I. MacBean, 1966. Harvard University Press.

Foreign Policy and Democratic Politics, by Kenneth N. Waltz (sponsored jointly with the Institute of War and Peace Studies, Columbia University), 1967. Little, Brown & Co.

Contemporary Military Strategy, by Morton H. Halperin, 1967. Little, Brown & Co.

Sino-Soviet Relations and Arms Control, ed. Morton H. Halperin (sponsored jointly with the East Asian Research Center), 1967. M.I.T. Press.

Africa and United States Policy, by Rupert Emerson, 1967. Prentice-Hall.

Elites in Latin America, edited by Seymour M. Lipset and Aldo Solari, 1967. Oxford University Press.

Europe's Postwar Growth, by Charles P. Kindleberger, 1967. Harvard University Press.

The Rise and Decline of the Cold War, by Paul Seabury, 1967. Basic Books.

Student Politics, ed. S.M. Lipset, 1967. Basic Books.

Pakistan's Development: Social Goals and Private Incentives, by Gustav F. Papanek, 1967. Harvard University Press.

Strike a Blow and Die: A Narrative of Race Relations in Colonial Africa, by George Simeon Mwase, ed. Robert I. Rotberg, 1967. Harvard University Press.

Party Systems and Voter Alignments, edited by Seymour M. Lipset and Stein Rokkan, 1967. Free Press.

Agrarian Socialism, by Seymour M. Lipset, revised edition, 1968. Doubleday Anchor.

Aid, Influence, and Foreign Policy, by Joan M. Nelson, 1968. The Macmillan Company.

Development Policy: Theory and Practice, edited by Gustav F. Papanek, 1968. Harvard University Press.

International Regionalism, by Joseph S. Nye, 1968. Little, Brown & Co.

Revolution and Counterrevolution, by Seymour M. Lipset, 1968. Basic Books.

Political Order in Changing Societies, by Samuel P. Huntington, 1968. Yale University Press.

The TFX Decision: McNamara and the Military, by Robert J. Art, 1968. Little, Brown & Co.

Korea: The Politics of the Vortex, by Gregory Henderson, 1968. Harvard University Press.

Political Development in Latin America, by Martin Needler, 1968. Random House.

The Precarious Republic, by Michael Hudson, 1968. Random House.

The Brazilian Capital Goods Industry, 1929-1964 (sponsored jointly with the Center for Studies in Education and Development), by Nathaniel H. Leff, 1968. John Wiley & Sons.

Economic Policy-Making and Development in Brazil, 1947-1964, by Nathaniel H. Leff, 1968. John Wiley & Sons.

Turmoil and Transition: Higher Education and Student Politics in India, edited by Philip G. Altbach, 1968. Lalvani Publishing House (Bombay).

German Foreign Policy in Transition, by Karl Kaiser, 1968. Oxford University Press.

Protest and Power in Black Africa, edited by Robert I. Rotberg, 1969. Oxford University Press.

Peace in Europe, by Karl E. Birnbaum, 1969. Oxford University Press.

The Process of Modernization: An Annotated Bibliography on the Sociocultural Aspects of Development, by John Brode, 1969. Harvard University Press.

Students in Revolt, edited by Seymour M. Lipset and Philip G. Altbach, 1969. Houghton Mifflin.

Agricultural Development in India's Districts: The Intensive Agricultural Districts Programme, by Dorris D. Brown, 1970. Harvard University Press.

Authoritarian Politics in Modern Society: The Dynamics of Established One-Party Systems, edited by Samuel P. Huntington and Clement H. Moore, 1970. Basic Books

Nuclear Diplomacy, by George H. Quester, 1970. Dunellen.

The Logic of Images in International Relations, by Robert Jervis, 1970. Princeton University Press.

Europe's Would-Be Polity, by Leon Lindberg and Stuart A. Scheingold, 1970. Prentice-Hall.

Taxation and Development: Lessons from Colombian Experience, by Richard M. Bird, 1970. Harvard University Press.

Lord and Peasant in Peru: A Paradigm of Political and Social Change, by F. LaMond Tullis, 1970. Harvard University Press.

The Kennedy Round in American Trade Policy: The Twilight of the GATT? by John W. Evans, 1971. Harvard University Press.

Korean Development: The Interplay of Politics and Economics, by David C. Cole and Princeton N. Lyman, 1971. Harvard University Press.

Development Policy II–The Pakistan Experience, edited by Walter P. Falcon and Gustav F. Papanek, 1971. Harvard University Press.

Higher Education in a Transitional Society, by Philip G. Altbach, 1971. Sindhu Publications (Bombay).

Studies in Development Planning, edited by Hollis B. Chenery, 1971. Harvard University Press.

Passion and Politics, by Seymour M. Lipset with Gerald Schaflander, 1971. Little, Brown & Co.

Political Mobilization of the Venezuelan Peasant, by John D. Powell, 1971. Harvard University Press.

Higher Education in India, edited by Amrik Singh and Philip Altbach, 1971. Oxford University Press (Delhi).

The Myth of the Guerrilla, by J. Bowyer Bell, 1971. Blond (London) and Knopf (New York).

International Norms and War between States: Three Studies in International Politics, by Kjell Goldmann, 1971. Published jointly by Läromedelsförlagen (Sweden) and the Swedish Institute of International Affairs.

Peace in Parts: Integration and Conflict in Regional Organization, by Joseph S. Nye, Jr., 1971. Little, Brown & Co.

Sovereignty at Bay: The Multinational Spread of U.S. Enterprise, by Raymond Vernon, 1971. Basic Books.

Defense Strategy for the Seventies (revision of *Contemporary Military Strategy*) by Morton H. Halperin, 1971. Little, Brown & Co.

Peasants Against Politics: Rural Organization in Brittany, 1911-1967, by Suzanne Berger, 1972. Harvard University Press.

Transnational Relations and World Politics, edited by Robert O. Keohane and Joseph S. Nye, Jr., 1972. Harvard University Press.

Latin American University Students: A Six-Nation Study, by Arthur Liebman, Kenneth N. Walker, and Myron Glazer, 1972. Harvard University Press.

The Politics of Land Reform in Chile, 1950-1970: Public Policy, Political Institutions and Social Change, by Robert R. Kaufman, 1972. Harvard University Press.

The Boundary Politics of Independent Africa, by Saadia Touval, 1972. Harvard University Press.

The Politics of Nonviolent Action, by Gene E. Sharp, 1973. Porter Sargent.

System 37 Viggen: Arms, Technology, and the Domestication of Glory, by Ingemar Dörfer, 1973. Universitetsforlaget (Oslo).

University Students and African Politics, by William John Hanna, 1974. Africana Publishing Company.

Organizing the Transnational: The Experience with Transnational Enterprise in Advanced Technology, by M.S. Hochmuth, 1974. Sijthoff (Leiden).

Becoming Modern, by Alex Inkeles and David H. Smith, 1974, Harvard University Press.

The United States and West Germany 1945-1973: A Study in Alliance Politics, by Roger Morgan (sponsored jointly with the Royal Institute of International Affairs), 1974. Oxford University Press.

Multinational Corporations and the Politics of Dependence: Copper in Chile, 1945-1973, by Theodore Moran, 1974. Princeton University Press.

The Andean Group: A Case Study in Economic Integration Among Developing Countries, by David Morawetz, 1974. M.I.T. Press.

Kenya: The Politics of Participation and Control, by Henry Bienen, 1974. Princeton University Press.

Land Reform and Politics: A Comparative Analysis, by Hung-chao Tai, 1974. University of California Press.

Big Business and the State:Changing Relations in Western Europe, edited by Raymond Vernon, 1974. Harvard University Press.

Economic Policymaking in a Conflict Society: The Argentine Case, by Richard D. Mallon and Juan V. Sourrouille, 1975. Harvard University Press.

New States in the Modern World, edited by Martin Kilson, 1975. Harvard University Press.

Revolutionary Civil War: The Elements of Victory and Defeat, by David Wilkinson, 1975. Page-Ficklin Publications.

Politics and the Migrant Poor in Mexico City, by Wayne A. Cornelius, 1975. Stanford University Press.

East Africa and the Orient: Cultural Syntheses in Pre-Colonial Times, ed. H. Neville Chittick and Robert I. Rotberg, 1975. Africana Publishing Company.

No Easy Choice: Political Participation in Developing Countries, by Samuel P. Huntington and Joan M. Nelson, 1976. Harvard University Press.

The Politics of International Monetary Reform—The Exchange Crisis, by Michael J. Brenner, 1976. Ballinger Publishing Co.

The International Politics of Natural Resources, by Zuhayr Mikdashi, 1976. Cornell University Press.

The Oil Crisis, edited by Raymond Vernon, 1976. W.W. Norton & Co.

Social Change and Political Participation in Turkey, by Ergun Ozbudun, 1976. Princeton University Press.

The Arabs, Israelis, and Kissinger: A Secret History of American Diplomacy in the Middle East, by Edward R.F. Sheehan, 1976. Reader's Digest Press.

Perception and Misperception in International Politics, by Robert Jervis, 1976. Princeton University Press.

Power and Interdependence, by Robert O. Keohane and Joseph S. Nye, Jr., 1977. Little, Brown.

Soldiers in Politics: Military Coups and Governments, by Eric Nordlinger, 1977. Prentice-Hall.

The Military and Politics in Modern Times: On Professionals, Praetorians, and Revolutionary Soldiers, by Amos Perlmutter, 1977. Yale University Press.

Bankers and Borders: The Case of the American Banks in Britain, by Janet Kelly, 1977. Ballinger Publishing Co.

Shattered Peace: The Origins of the Cold War and the National Security State, by Daniel Yergin, 1977. Houghton Mifflin.

Storm Over the Multinationals: The Real Issues, by Raymond Vernon, 1977. Harvard University Press.

Political Generations and Political Development, ed. Richard J. Samuels, 1977. Lexington Books.

Cuba: Order and Revolution in the Twentieth Century, by Jorge I. Dominguez, 1978. Harvard University Press.

Raw Materials Investments and American Foreign Policy, by Stephen D. Krasner, 1978. Princeton University Press.

Commodity Conflict: The Political Economy of International Commodity Negotiations, by L.N. Rangarajan, 1978. Cornell University Press and Croom Helm (London).

Israel: Embattled Ally, by Nadav Safran, 1978. Harvard University Press.

Access to Power: Political Participation by the Urban Poor in Developing Nations, by Joan M. Nelson, 1979. Princeton University Press.

The Quest for Self-Determination, by Dov Ronen, 1979. Yale University Press.

The Rational Peasant: The Political Economy of Rural Society in Vietnam, by Samuel L. Popkin, 1979. University of California Press.

Legislative-Executive Relations and the Politics of United States Foreign Economics Policy 1929-1979, by Robert Pastor, 1980. University of California Press.

Insurrection and Loyalty: The Breakdown of the Spanish American Empire, by Jorge Dominguez, 1980. Harvard University Press.

Standing Guard: The Protection of Foreign Investment, by Charles Lipson, 1980. University of California Press.

The Collapse of Welfare Reform: Political Institutions, Policy and the Poor in Canada and the United States, by Christopher Leman, 1980. M.I.T. Press.

Palestinian Society and Politics, by Joel S. Migdal et al., 1980. Princeton University Press.

Weak States in the International System, by Michael Handel, 1980. Frank Cass, London.

HARVARD STUDIES IN INTERNATIONAL AFFAIRS*

30. *Israel's Political-Military Doctrine*, by Michael I. Handel, 1973. 101 pp. $3.75.
31. *Italy, NATO and the European Community: The Interplay of Foreign Policy and Domestic Politics*, by Primo Vannicelli, 1974. 67 + x pp. $3.75.
32. *The Choice of Technology in Developing Countries: Some Cautionary Tales*, by C. Peter Timmer, John W. Thomas, Louis T. Wells, Jr., and David Morawetz, 1975. 114 pp. $3.95.
33. *The International Role of the Communist Parties of Italy and France*, by Donald L.M. Blackmer and Annie Kriegel, 1975. 67 + x pp. $3.50.
34. *The Hazards of Peace: A European View of Detente*, by Juan Cassiers, 1976. 94 pp. $3.50.
35. *Oil and the Middle East War: Europe in the Energy Crisis*, by Robert J. Lieber, 1976. 75 + x pp. $3.45.
37. *Climatic Change and World Affairs*, by Crispin Tickell, 1977. 78 pp. $3.95.
38. *Conflict and Violence in Lebanon: Confrontation in the Middle East*, by Walid Khalidi, 1979. 217 pp. $12.95, cloth; $6.95, paper.
39. *Diplomatic Dispute: U.S. Conflict with Iran, Japan, and Mexico*, by Robert L. Paarlberg, Ed, Eul Y. Park, and Donald L. Wyman, 1979. 168 pp. $11.95, cloth; $5.95, paper.
40. *Commandos and Politicians: Elite Military Units in Modern Democracies*, by Eliot A. Cohen, 1978. 136 pp. $8.95, cloth; $3.95, paper.
41. *Yellow Earth, Green Jade: Constants in Chinese Political Mores*, by Simon de Beaufort 1979. 90 pp. $3.95, paper.
42. *The Future of North America: Canada, the United States, and Quebec Nationalism*, Elliot J. Feldman and Neil Nevitte, eds., 1979. 378 pp. $13.95, cloth; $6.95, paper.
43. *The Dependence Dilemma: Gasoline Consumption and America's Security*, Daniel Yergin, Ed., 1980. 167 pp. $4.95, paper.
44. *The Diplomacy of Surprise: Hitler, Nixon, Sadat*, by Michael I. Handel, 1980. 320 pp. $16.00 cloth, $9.00, paper. Publication date August 1980.

*Available from Harvard University Center for International Affairs, 1737 Cambridge Street, Cambridge, Mass. 02138.
†Out of print. Reprints may be ordered from AMS Press, Inc., 56 East 13th Street, New York, N.Y. 10003

ORDER FORM

Harvard Center for International Affairs
Publications Office
1737 Cambridge Street, Cambridge, Mass. 02138

Please send me _____ copies of THE DEPENDENCE DILEMMA

  1-4 copies $4.95 each / $1.00 for postage and handling
  5-14 copies $4.45 each / $2.00 for postage and handling
  15-24 copies $3.95 each / $2.00 for postage and handling
  25 or more $3.45 each / $2.00 for postage and handling

☐ Payment enclosed. Make check payable to Harvard University.
☐ Bill me

NAME _____

ADDRESS _____

CITY _____

STATE _____ ZIP _____

Harvard Center for International Affairs
Publications Office
1737 Cambridge Street, Cambridge, Mass. 02138

Please send me the Harvard Studies in International Affairs checked below. (Indicate number of copies.)

_____ 43. THE DEPENDENCE DILEMMA: GASOLINE CONSUMPTION AND AMERICA'S SECURITY, Daniel Yergin, Ed., 180 pp. Paper, $4.95; 1980.

Cloth _____ 42. THE FUTURE OF NORTH AMERICA: CANADA, THE
Paper _____ UNITED STATES, AND QUEBEC NATIONALISM, by Elliot J. Feldman and Neil Nevitte, eds., 378 pp. Cloth, $13.95; paper, $6.95; 1979.

_____ 41. YELLOW EARTH, GREEN JADE: CONSTANTS IN CHINESE POLITICAL MORES, by Simon de Beaufort, 90 pp. Paper, $3.95; 1979.

Cloth _____ 40. COMMANDOS AND POLITICIANS: ELITE MILITARY UNITS
Paper _____ IN MODERN DEMOCRACIES, by Eliot A. Cohen, 136 pp. Cloth, $8.95; paper, $3.95; 1978.

Cloth _____ 39. DIPLOMATIC DISPUTE: U.S. CONFLICT WITH IRAN, JAPAN,
Paper _____ AND MEXICO, by Robert L. Paarlberg, Ed., Eul Y. Park, and Donald L. Wyman, 173 pp. Cloth, $11.95; paper, $5.95; 1979.

Cloth _____ 38. CONFLICT AND VIOLENCE IN LEBANON: CONFRONTA-
Paper _____ TION IN THE MIDDLE EAST, by Walid Khalidi, 217 pp. Cloth, $12.95; paper, $6.95; 1980.

_____ 37. CLIMATIC CHANGE AND WORLD AFFAIRS, by Crispin Tickell, 78 pp. Paper, $3.95.

_____ 35. OIL AND THE MIDDLE EAST WAR: EUROPE IN THE ENERGY CRISIS, by Robert J. Leiber, 75 + vii pp. Paper, $3.95.

_____ 34. THA HAZARDS OF PEACE: A EUROPEAN VIEW OF DE-TENTE, by Juan Cassiers, 94 pp. Paper, $3.50.

_____ 33. THE INTERNATIONAL ROLE OF THE COMMUNIST PAR-TIES OF FRANCE AND ITALY, by Donald L.M. Blackmer and Annie Kriegel, 67 + x pp. Paper, $3.50.

_____ 31. ITALY, NATO, AND THE EUROPEAN COMMUNITY: THE INTERPLAY OF FOREIGN POLICY AND DOMESTIC POLI-TICS, by Primo Vanicelli, 67 + x pp. Paper, $3.75.

_____ 29. CONFLICT REGULATION IN DIVIDED SOCIETIES, by Eric A. Nordlinger, 141 pp. Paper, $4.95.

FORTHCOMING PUBLICATION

44. *The Diplomacy of Surprise: Hitler, Nixon, Sadat,* by Michael I. Handel, 1980. 320 pp. $16.00 cloth, $9.00, paper. Publication date August 1980.

Harvard Center for International Affairs
Publications Office   1737 Cambridge Street, Cambridge, Mass. 02138

Please send me the book(s) checked on this form.

☐ I enclose check for $_____

   (We pay postage and handling on prepaid orders)

☐ Please bill me

Name _____

Address _____

_____